Living in a Straw House Built by Undiagnosed Neurodivergence

A Family's Memoir and Framework for Weathering Storms with Compassion and Clarity

Lish Greiner

Living in the Straw House That Neurodivergence Built

© 2025 Lish Greiner
All rights reserved.

No part of this book may be reproduced, distributed, or transmitted
in any form or by any means, including photocopying, recording, or other electronic or mechanical methods, without the prior written permission of the publisher, except in the case of brief quotations used in critical reviews and certain other noncommercial uses permitted by copyright law.

For permission requests, contact:
audhdlish@gmail.com
or through the author's website at:
www.neurodivergentcompass.com

Cover design and interior layout by Lish Greiner

Printed in the United States of America.

ISBN: 9798275734331

Dedications:

To Keleigh:
You were gifted to me to change this world, and you have.

To Linda:
My forever supporter, this life wouldn't be possible without you.

To Cray, Danielle & Sarah:
Thank you for loving me, even when it's hard and I'm weird.

To the many other "kids" in my life:
Thanks for guiding me along the way.

"I didn't come this far to only come this far."
— Unknown

Table of Contents

Part One — Our Family's Memoir	1
Chapter 1 - My Straw House Begins to Buckle	2
Chapter 2: My Straw House Collapses	13
Chapter 3: After Collapse, It Gets Better — But Also Worse	28
Chapter 4: Keleigh's Room Keeps Collapsing	43
Chapter 5: Things Finally Start to ADD Up	58
Chapter 6: My Second Burnout	68
Chapter 7: The Rebuild — This Time I Use a Blueprint and Bricks	80
Part Two — Blueprint for Weathering the Storms of Neurodivergent Life	92
Alexithymia	97
Auditory Processing Differences (APD)	103
Bottom-Up Processing	108
Communication Styles and Language Differences	117
Difficulty (or inability) to Change, Transition or Shift	119
Eating & Food	127
Echolalia	132
Emotional Dysregulation	133
Executive Dysfunction	137
Invisible Disability Paradox	161
Interest-Based Systems	162
Interoception	166

Lack of Intuitive Social Processing	170
Late Diagnosis / Misdiagnosis	173
Masking & Camouflaging	175
Monotropism/Hyperfocus	181
Neurodivergent System Overload – Overwhelm, Meltdowns, Shutdowns, and Burnout	190
Object and People Impermanence	210
Proprioception Challenges	229
Rejection Sensitive Dysphoria (RSD)	230
Routine	237
Sensory Processing Differences (SPD)	238
Sleep Irregularities	245
Social-Relational Layers	246
Special Interest	248
Spiky Skills	250
Stimming	250
Strong Sense of Justice	252
Swiss Cheese Memory	255
The Paradox of Being Neurodivergent	257
The Weight of Being Misunderstood	259
Time Blindness	260
Closing Thoughts	266

A Note on Triggers

Before we begin, I want to acknowledge the sensitive nature of what's to come. This book openly discusses topics that may be difficult or painful for some readers, including:

- Suicidal thoughts and ideation
- Self-harm
- Miscarriage
- Partner physical and emotional abuse
- Parental neglect
- Traumatic birth experience

I believe it's crucial to share these parts of the story openly and honestly. Sharing our experiences can help us understand the profound emotional toll of living in a world that often doesn't see or accommodate us.

If these topics are hard for you right now, please know it's okay to step away. Come back when you're ready. Take care of yourself in whatever way you need to.

Author's Note

This is a true story, told from my perspective and to the best of my memory. I have changed or omitted the names and identifying details of some individuals to protect their privacy.

This book reflects my lived experience. It includes difficult moments, including trauma, abuse, and mental health struggles. These stories are not told to harm anyone, but to give voice to realities that are often hidden and to help others feel less alone in their own chaos, confusion, and healing.

These events are portrayed as I experienced them. While others may have different memories of the same events, I've written this narrative with care, integrity, and honesty.

This is not a book about blame. It's a book about understanding.

Preface

When my daughter, Keleigh, was three years old, she told me she wanted to die.

It was a shocking sentence to hear, but in some ways, it made sense.

We didn't yet have the words to describe her experience, but Keleigh had struggled since birth. She never slept. She never settled. She was always crying, always on edge, always dysregulated. Even though she roughly hit her milestones, nothing ever felt quite right. Every part of life was a battle.

So, while it was horrifying to hear a small child say those words, it also... fit.

Suicidality wasn't foreign to me. I grew up with it. My family has a long history of suicidal thoughts and ideation. At least one of my sisters would regularly say she didn't want to be alive. I had lived alongside that pain for so long, I was familiar with it.

I don't remember exactly why Keleigh said it that day. We were in the car. She was buckled in her car seat, struggling with some everyday frustration—and I *lost it*.

I screamed. I yelled at my tiny, beautiful child. My reaction was completely over the top. I can't recall exactly what I said, but I know I told her, over and over, to never, ever say that again.

I was triggered deep in my nervous system, my brain flashing through a lifetime of memories— and I feared my daughter might walk the same painful path as my sister.

Of course, my reaction didn't have a positive impact. If it had, this would be a very short book.

That was the first time she said she didn't want to be alive, and it wouldn't be the last. I don't know how many times she said it over the next decade—hundreds, maybe thousands. It became a constant undercurrent in our lives. And it wasn't just that. It was everything. Her struggles only escalated with time.

This book is about neurodiversity—specifically our family's experience of Autism, ADHD, and PDA (Pathological Demand Avoidance, sometimes reframed as a Persistent Drive for Autonomy). When Autism and ADHD overlap, it's known as AuDHD.

It's also about late diagnosis and the trauma of not knowing.

For many years, I didn't have the language to explain what was happening to my daughter, and certainly not for myself.

Our house usually looked fine, or at least good enough, from the outside. But it was never truly functional. We were always on the edge of collapse, trying to survive a storm we couldn't name, taking shelter in a fragile straw house built by all of us: a group of undiagnosed neurodivergents doing our best with no blueprint or framework.

It took decades to understand why everything had always felt so impossibly hard.

My goal in writing this is simple:
To tell our story so others know they're not alone.
To put words to experiences that often go unspoken.

To replace misunderstandings with some kind of understanding.

To let families like mine know that what they're going through is real, and more common than we're led to believe.

Many of us suffer in silence; confused, overwhelmed, and convinced we're failing. We're given parenting handbooks that aren't relevant to our lives. We're given advice that only serves to deepen our shame. We're left to navigate systems that were never designed for brains like ours, or for children like ours.

I know how isolating it all feels. I also know how healing it is to finally hear your truth reflected in someone else's words. Telling our stories is how we release the weight of our guilt and shame.

It's how we reclaim our truth from a world that doesn't always understand us.

Every story we tell pulls back the curtain a little more on what it means to live in a neurodivergent family—raw, beautiful, chaotic, and full of love that doesn't always look the way people expect it to.

It's also how we begin to shift the systems that can't hold us. Not just schools and doctors and public services, but the cultural systems that reward conformity and punish difference.

Those systems won't change if we keep pretending that we're fine. If we keep hiding.

Our stories become a kind of blueprint—not a perfect one, not a step-by-step guide—but a living, breathing map drawn from lived experience. A framework for surviving when the world isn't built for your wiring. A way to build better shelter. A way to make sure fewer people weather the storm alone.

I believe Keleigh was born with a purpose—not to carry the weight of what came before her, but to help break those detrimental patterns. Somewhere along the way, without either of us knowing it, she became the key that unlocked my own understanding of myself. Through her, I began to see long-hidden parts of my life. And in helping her find her way, I began—at last—to find mine.

＊Part One — Our Family's Memoir＊

Chapter 1 - My Straw House Begins to Buckle

Before I could name our experiences:

The day my life changed forever, but also didn't, was the day I gave birth to Keleigh. It's fair to say that most people remember the day their children were born. For me, much of that day is lost in a haze, but a few things stand out with painful clarity.

The pregnancy itself was uneventful. I carried Keleigh long enough to be induced. My labor was mostly uneventful, too, until it wasn't.

The nurses became concerned that Keleigh was in distress. They called in the doctor and prepared me for an emergency c-section. But the doctor decided there wasn't enough time. I was nine centimeters dilated, and he said it would be faster to deliver her in the room than to scrub-in for surgery. So that's what they did.

A vacuum was placed on her head, and they suctioned her head out. In that instant, two terrible things became clear: the umbilical cord was wrapped twice around her neck, and I was experiencing extreme shoulder dystocia. Shoulder dystocia is a medical emergency, where the pelvis doesn't open appropriately, and the baby's shoulders cannot pass through. It can be fatal for both mother and baby.

In that moment, everything changed. The doctor told me, calmly but firmly, that it was about to get really hectic, and I needed to listen only to his voice. A nurse pressed the call button for help. A voice crackled over the speaker: "Can I help you?" My nurse screamed back, "I need help in here!" I could feel the panic in her voice. As a nurse, I knew that when a nurse panicked, the situation was of the utmost seriousness.

The room exploded with people. Two nurses jumped onto the bed and began pushing on my stomach (in what I now know as an effort to push her underneath my pelvis). The doctor told me to push as hard and as long as I could and not to stop until he said so. I pushed until the edges of my vision went black. I was losing consciousness, I don't know what happened or how much time passed, but somehow, they got her out.

I remember seeing her limp, grayish body rushed out of the room. I turned and saw my sister, who had been in the room, on her knees, begging and screaming to God to save Keleigh's life. Keleigh's APGAR score was zero. There were no signs of life.

Someone told me Keleigh had been resuscitated. She was breathing and miraculously seemed mostly unharmed; no broken bones, no apparent injuries from her traumatic entry into the world, but she had to stay under the nurses' constant watch in the nursery for hours afterward. It was eight hours or so before I was finally allowed to hold her.

There's one part I remember so clearly that it still feels too raw to say out loud, even now. For more than a decade I didn't tell anyone, and to this day I've only told my wife and a therapist. Before I held Keleigh, I could see her through the nursery glass, and I didn't feel anything. I had always been told that when you see your child for the first time, you feel this overwhelming rush of love. Your heart expands, and suddenly you experience a love like you've never felt before. But I felt... nothing. I thought maybe it was birth trauma, and that when I held her, I would feel love. But when I finally had her in my arms, I still didn't feel it. I surmised that eventually I would have some sort of tidal wave of love wash over me, or something like that, and that was kind of that. I buried the shame of that moment deep down inside.

Eventually, Keleigh passed all the medical requirements and was released from the nursery to be in the room with us. It was pretty late, and I still hadn't slept or rested, which turned out to be a mistake—she cried for the entire night. My first night as a mother, and my baby cried the entire night. It was a harsh reality and a sign of things to come. She cried that night and for the next thirteen years. She was restless, inconsolable, and unsettled. That was just the beginning.

For some context, I was a 29-year-old nurse, and I had just bought my first home. I thought I was in a "good" place, and if nothing else, I had at least broken the cycle of poverty that I had grown up in. At the time, I was in a relationship with a man who seemed like a good person.

Very early on, I wanted to go back to work. I had planned to stay home longer, and I had the time and resources to do that, but being home was very hard for me, and work seemed like it would be easier, so her father became a stay-at-home dad for a little while. I recall feeling like a failure because a mom should want to stay with her baby. I also remember wondering how in the world did our grandmas stay home with all their babies. I know they didn't have too much of a choice, but still, I just didn't understand how it had been possible.

When Keleigh was maybe four months old, I got pregnant with twins and lost them both midway through the pregnancy. My memory of this time is incredibly poor, but not long after that, the "good guy" and I broke up.

This was a turning point in my life. My straw house had been buckling here and there, but now there was a storm moving in, and my straw house was in its direct path. What followed was both strange and, sadly, not unfamiliar. I was hit with the harsh reality that Keleigh's dad would never see her or me again.

I had believed he was a good guy; kind, caring, and a good dad. I truly thought we would co-parent peacefully, that things would be civil, even friendly. I could not have been more wrong.

The shift in how he treated me was abrupt—like a switch had been flipped. He and his family went from warm and involved to cold, erratic, and deeply invasive. Practically overnight, the man I thought was a good dad transformed into someone unrecognizable—doing things so petty and cruel they felt almost performative, like something out of a movie. It was disorienting. Surreal. I couldn't make sense of what was happening or how it had happened so fast. I kept trying to reconcile this new version of him with the person I thought I knew, but I just couldn't. My brain couldn't process that both versions could be real. It felt impossible. I could not believe it.

And yet, it was oddly familiar. I had experienced this kind of whiplash before, when someone I trusted became someone I didn't recognize. But even with that history, I still couldn't believe it was happening. If someone had told me this would be the outcome, I would have bet my life against it.

The state of disbelief I was in cannot be overstated. I kept reaching out to him, calling, messaging, desperate to make my reality untrue. Once, I even showed up at his mother's house with Keleigh in my arms, hoping to talk and understand. Instead, I was threatened with the police if I didn't leave the porch.

This may sound like a typical story of being bad at dating. A typical dad-leaves-mom-with-baby kind of story. And yes, I was bad at dating, but it was more than that. What sits beneath is a foundation built from straw.

Now that I have the right words:

Looking back at this snippet of my life, I see glaring signs of neurodivergence. When Keleigh was born and I didn't experience the instant rush of love I had read about in books or seen in movies, the kind where everything else fades and your heart swells with joy, I didn't really know what to think. Because I didn't have the right words to describe my experience, I developed a chorus of quiet, brutal narratives about myself. I believed I was a bad mother. That I was broken. That something was deeply wrong with me. That I didn't deserve to be a mother at all. I surmised that these were the reasons why I lost my twins. I believed I was cold, unfit, and incapable of being a good mom. I carried those stories with me for years. But actually, it wasn't any of those things. It was because I experience alexithymia.

Alexithymia is a common trait in neurodivergent people, where emotions don't come easily or show up in ways we expect. It's not a lack of love or empathy. It's not that we don't care, although that is often the way it is perceived by others—and by ourselves, if we aren't familiar with the concept. It's that we don't have the words, or the gut-feeling connections, for what we're feeling in those moments. It's like being caught in a storm with no name, no warning, and no way to describe what's pelting your skin. You know something is definitely happening, but you can't make sense of it or have the right words to describe it. Sometimes it takes days, weeks, or even months to understand what we were feeling in a given moment, if we ever manage to understand it at all. That delay or absence can be profoundly disorienting. This experience isn't on most people's radar because it isn't often discussed. And when it's not on our radar, we're left to assume the worst about ourselves. We're left to believe that we are in the wrong.

At the time, I didn't know any of this. I just carried a quiet, heavy shame. I thought I couldn't love my child. But alexithymia doesn't erase your love, it's just different from the neurotypical experience we always hear about. My love for Keleigh has always been there, even if I didn't know how to see it—I was looking through a lens not meant for me. That moment of clarity never came; not like a wave, not like a lightbulb. I didn't get the sudden rush or a0AZ deep knowing. What I got was a long road, and I clawed my way along it on my hands and knees, through thick mud and thorny brush, bloodied and bruised. I showed up even when I had nothing to give, and it wasn't enough. It wasn't the kind of love people recognize or celebrate. It didn't look like anything most people would call love. But it was what I had. And I gave it my best. Every single day. Even when I was empty. Even during the parts I can't remember. Even when I was doing it incredibly poorly, it was still my best. That was my love; it just didn't look the way I'd been taught to expect.

The neurodivergent aspect of relationships is a little more clouded than other parts of my story. Now that I have the right words, I understand there were layers I couldn't see at the time. The absence of intuitive social processing is one of the most invisible, misunderstood aspects of being neurodivergent—especially for people with autism, ADHD, or both. It means not naturally absorbing or interpreting the unwritten rules of social life that many neurotypical people seem to just know. It's not easy to describe, but I'll do my best.

Many ND folks, myself included, struggle with reading social cues and understanding the unspoken dynamics in relationships (of all kinds). We tend to take things literally and believe people at face value. We don't always have that internal "radar" for manipulation or danger that some neurotypicals seem to carry. We also often mask or people-please—sometimes to the point of losing ourselves entirely—because we've been conditioned to earn safety or belonging by being easy, likable, or accommodating.

We also have a deep capacity for empathy and loyalty, and when combined with the aforementioned attributes, this can make us targets for people who can exploit or manipulate those traits. It's not because we're "weak" or "naive"—it's a mismatch between how our brains process relationships and how those around us may exploit that difference.

That made me more vulnerable than I realized. That kind of vulnerability can be read loud and clear. In my experience, people tend to have one of two responses to this phenomenon: they either feel a desire to protect me, or they see an opening to exploit or take advantage. Keleigh's father was the second kind.

The sad reality of being an undiagnosed neurodivergent person is that the lack of understanding creates these situations far too often. In the story of what happened between Keleigh's father and I, all the signs were there. They weren't subtle or quietly lingering in the background. They were glaring, bright, flashing, and comically obvious. If I told you the whole story, every chaotic, wildly obvious red flag, you'd likely be completely bewildered that I didn't see them. You might even struggle to believe me; the story is that outlandish. And honestly, I wish that were the case. I wish I were exaggerating or making it up somehow. But I'm not. It would be laughable if it weren't so devastating.

Keleigh's dad was involved in things that should have raised every alarm in me. I didn't see them and excuse them: I genuinely didn't *see* them at all. It wasn't just a matter of reconciling facts with my beliefs about him. The information barely registered at all. I was simply trying to survive, navigating each day the best I could without realizing that other people weren't struggling so hard just to exist. Most things didn't stick with me long enough to piece together a bigger picture. I didn't understand relationships the way I thought I did. I didn't have the framework to make sense of them. I certainly didn't have any reference for my absence of intuitive social processing. So, I kept moving forward, believing he was a good guy, believing we would co-parent, believing everything was fine—until it wasn't. And when it all fell apart, I was completely shocked.

That shock, that inability to believe what was happening even as it was happening, is one of the clearest ways I now see my neurodivergence at play (and it will show up again and again throughout my story). I wasn't willfully ignorant. I wasn't in denial. I was operating without a map and compass, without even knowing I was lost. The chaos and confusion that followed weren't just about heartbreak or betrayal; they were about a fundamental mismatch between my brain's interpretation of relationships and how the world around me actually works; the absence of intuitive social processing.

Neurotypical people talk about gut feelings, red flags, or instincts—but I don't have access to any of that. I can't read between the lines. I believe what I'm told because that's how my brain works. I take things literally, even when they don't add up. Sometimes, I may have a vague sense that something is perhaps a little off, but without a clear, logical explanation, it's easy for me to not quite comprehend it, especially when I'm already barely scraping by without even realizing. All this lands me in one of two places: either I assume the problem is me, not the situation, not the other person, just me, or I assume this must be how life is. That this is what relationships are like. That everyone else is quietly struggling like me. And because I believe we're all living in the same world, I don't think to question it. I just keep going. I don't realize I'm living in a straw house—one strong gust away from serious structural problems.

I kept reaching out, trying to undo what was happening, trying to force reality back into the version that made sense. I couldn't believe the situation with Keleigh's dad was real—because I didn't yet understand that I hadn't ever fully understood him or our relationship at all. I hadn't seen it, not because I refused to, but because I didn't know how. That level of unknowing, that gap between what was happening and what I could process, was profoundly disorienting.

I was completely disorientated. That's what it looks like to live without the right words, the right understanding, and the right tools. It's like trying to solve a puzzle with missing pieces and no picture on the box. In the absence of clarity, I often assume the best—because I don't know any other way.

It's strange, isn't it? That I instinctively assume the best in others, but the worst in myself. Like I trust their intentions more than I trust my own perceptions.

Even before I knew I was neurodivergent, I carried this quiet, persistent sense that something about me was off—or at least, different. I was always confused, but I wouldn't have called it confusion at the time. It just felt like... noise. Fog. Static. Like trying to tune into a world that was broadcasting on a frequency I could never quite tune into.

I didn't have the language or framework to understand what I was feeling. So, I did what many of us do—I bounced between two extremes. Sometimes, I was sure I was the problem. Everyone else seemed to move through the world without fog and friction. Other times, I swung the other way, deciding *they* were the weird ones—and I was the one seeing clearly. I didn't know it yet, but both responses were me trying to make sense of something deeper: I was living in a world that didn't match my wiring.

This part of my story is not meant to place blame on Keleigh's father. I played as much a role in the pattern as he did. He has his own story, his own struggles, and his own pain to work through. We've never heard from him since that time, but I'm grateful that whatever he was working through no longer touches me or my daughter.

This was only the beginning. This story gets much worse before it gets better. The straw house I was living in didn't collapse during this time, but the winds were picking up. The walls had started to buckle, the foundation was beginning to falter, and the roof was starting to sag. I began to feel a draft inside. It wasn't a house I built alone; my family and ancestors had built it with me from the only materials we had. Neurodivergence runs through all of us, unnamed and unspoken, shaping how we loved, survived, and struggled. We didn't have the blueprints or the right tools. We did the best we could with straw. And for a while, for me, it held good enough. But the storm was coming.

Chapter 2: My Straw House Collapses

So there I was, 30 years old, with a baby, no sign of the father, a demanding nursing career, and no family around. What came next was a blur—some of the worst years I've ever lived through. It was the first time I truly experienced what I now know as neurodivergent burnout, though I didn't have the words for it back then. The damage it caused to both Keleigh and me, lives on as an echo of our traumatic story.

Before I could name our experience:

I can't fully describe how profoundly I suffered and how completely I stopped functioning. Even as I try, I know my words can't capture it.

I couldn't take care of my baby. I couldn't take care of myself. Keleigh and I were both in constant states of yelling, screaming, crying. Which came first? I don't have any idea, but I know it wasn't good.

Mornings were beyond chaotic. Getting ready for the day wasn't just hard, it was utter mayhem; several hours of intense volatility, with me and my tiny child both screaming, crying, rocking, and panicking. The mornings were marked with relentless intense reactivity and crying. For years, it was devastating chaos every morning.

Showering and the steps of getting ready felt incredibly heavy. Not just tiring or inconvenient, but like pushing through invisible molasses, every single day. The weight of it all was enormous, and with no clear reason.

Getting dressed has always been a struggle for me. And now I wasn't just dressing myself; I was dressing a baby, too. A baby who, every morning, seemed impossible to dress. I assumed she was being difficult and that I was bad at it.

What would be a twenty minute routine for most people took us two or three hours, every day. We left the house already depleted, already broken down. We started every day defeated.

I *did* have a vague sense that something was off. But I didn't truly grasp how far from "normal" our mornings really were. I thought everyone else felt this way, and that I was just handling it worse than they were.

At work I did well enough. In many ways I excelled, but in some ways I didn't. There was something about it that I was good at and in control of myself. I didn't experience extreme emotional volatility like I did at home. Most days, I would try to stay there longer than necessary, as I figured that was better for Keleigh. I had an inkling that it felt a little better to be at work and not experiencing the extreme volatility that I was at home. Even though work was hard, it was a different kind of hard.

After a long day of work, I usually came home and collapsed into what I assumed was just ordinary exhaustion—if I thought about it at all. Most days, I did the bare minimum: maybe I'd grab chicken nuggets from a drive-thru and put on a movie for Keleigh before crashing. But sometimes I couldn't even manage that.

There are nights from that time that are nothing but a blur—marked by crying, hysteria, and more or less passing out. There were mornings when I woke up and realized I hadn't fed Keleigh. Or myself. Most of the time, I was too tired to speak. I couldn't make dinner. I couldn't *move*.

Sometimes, I would just sit there on the couch, empty, while Keleigh was in full-blown distress: screaming, crying, hitting her head, pulling her hair, thrashing her body, holding her breath, shaking violently. And I would sit there—staring blankly at the TV or just a wall. Sometimes, I even fell asleep while she was screaming.

Other times, I'd break. I'm not sure who mirrored who. Sometimes I cried or screamed back. Not words, just sound. Sometimes words like *stop* or *shut up*—raw desperation, not cruelty. Sometimes I locked myself in the bathroom, sobbing, while my one-year-old screamed on the other side of the door.

This was our normal.

The house itself was a disaster. Literally trashed. Once, a friend came over unannounced. She stood frozen in the front room and called out to me. Her voice shook. When I answered from the back of the house, she exhaled sharply and said, 'Oh,

I thought your house had been broken into and ransacked." That's how bad it was.

As was my pattern at the time, I got into another relationship—this time with a woman—who was also deeply unhealthy and dealing with her own struggles. She was mentally and physically abusive to me, often violently, and sometimes in front of Keleigh. Again, I did have some sense it was wrong, but I just thought, "Oh, maybe this is what relationships are like sometimes."

Internally, I drifted between feeling completely blank—numb—and what I could only describe back then as having "flight of ideas," a term I remembered from nursing school.

My mind would race with scattered, overwhelming thoughts. Mostly, though, I just remember feeling ashamed. I was confused a lot, but I didn't realize it—I thought this was just how life worked. I remember thinking over and over that I must be a terrible mom. And that part didn't make sense to me. Nothing in my life before motherhood suggested I'd be bad at it. I had always wanted to be a mom. I pictured it as something natural and intuitive. But now I couldn't connect the dots between the love I wanted to feel and the chaos I was experiencing daily.

I remember constantly promising myself that tomorrow I'd do better. That I'd try harder, be calmer and more patient. That I'd make a real meal, clean the house, play with Keleigh the way other moms played with their children. But every day, I failed. I believed I could do all these things if I only tried harder. I don't know if it was hope or delusion that kept me making those promises—but I made them anyway, every single day.

I felt like I had absolutely no control over myself—my voice, my reactions, my energy.

I thought I was lazy. Bad at keeping a house. Maybe a little odd. I did notice a difference between how I was at work and how I was at home, but I didn't really question it. I didn't question anything, really. I just assumed this must be life. That everyone must be quietly struggling like this. And honestly, even if I'd wanted to figure it out, I didn't have the bandwidth. I was barely clinging to life—and I didn't even know it.

After roughly two years of this, I began seeing a man who was also in a relationship with someone else. At the time, I knew and believed with absolute certainty that he loved me.

I became pregnant. And he was furious.

He begged me to have an abortion. Pleaded, pressured, pushed. But that didn't feel right for me. The last time I ever saw him, he showed up at my house, desperate to change my mind. I don't remember too much, but an argument must have ensued. I collapsed on the floor, sobbing uncontrollably. He stepped over me on his way out, paused, looked down, and with cold, biting anger said: *"You're already fucking up one child, and now you're just going to fuck up another one."*

And then he left.

 I never saw him again.

It was another shock to the system—another moment when my internal world couldn't make sense of what was happening. Reality and my perception clashed so violently, it felt impossible to hold them simultaneously. I thought I knew him, so what was unfolding didn't compute. Just like before, I couldn't reconcile what I was experiencing with what I believed to be true. It simply didn't make sense.

The pregnancy ended in a very early miscarriage.

This description of those years still feels somewhat vague. Each day bled into the next. I don't specifically remember holidays. I don't remember milestones. I don't remember what year certain things happened. The only real markers were the crying, screaming, and all-round dysregulation, not because they particularly stood out, but because they formed the rhythm of our life.

Now That I Have the Right Words:

I now understand that I was living in a straw house built by neurodivergence, in an environment that was never meant for a straw house. The fragile walls were no match for the tornado alley I found myself in—storm after storm, tearing me down. I understand now that what I was experiencing during those years wasn't me being a bad mom or a messy person. It was neurodivergent overwhelm, meltdown, shutdown and burnout. I didn't have those words back then, but now they've given me a blueprint to finally understand what was happening, so I can shore up the walls, improve the foundation and weather the storms, or build a straw house in a better environment. Or build a whole new house from bricks!

What I thought was just feeling tired or stressed was actually autistic (neurodivergent) burnout. It was a complete collapse of my ability to function. At the time, I didn't have the language for it, but now I understand what was happening on a neurological level.

I like to think of neurodivergence as a spectrum of oven knobs (stick with me here). Each knob represents a different trait or sensitivity, and for every neurodivergent person, those knobs are set differently. They can shift based on environment, stress, or how many resources (or "spoons") we have available.

During this time, all my knobs were cranked too high. The traits I'd always carried—sensory sensitivity, executive dysfunction, emotional overwhelm, etc—were all pushed to their max. My brain and body were so overloaded, even the simplest tasks became impossible.

What appeared on the outside as anger, rage, exhaustion, or zoning out was actually my nervous system in survival mode. I was experiencing constant overwhelm, shutdowns and meltdowns. These weren't character flaws; they were neurological responses to living in a world that didn't accommodate my needs.

I now understand that I cycled through all the survival states: fight, when I screamed back at Keleigh, flight, when I locked myself in the bathroom and freeze, and when I zoned out completely, often while she was also melting down. That zoning out? I now know it's called dissociation.

My days were filled with sensory overload, executive dysfunction, and a constant undercurrent of anxiety and shame. I can see that the volatility in our mornings—those hours of screaming and chaos—wasn't just because I was failing. It was the collision of two overwhelmed, dysregulated nervous systems. I didn't understand how profoundly executive dysfunction, sensory overwhelm and burnout were driving my actions or inactions. What felt like personal failure was my brain and body trying to survive in a world that outweighed my abilities.

At work, there was clear structure and routine; everything was black and white. There were rules, and I knew how to follow them. Everything was easier to mask and manage. I had scripts and roles to play. I looked and even felt somewhat put together.

Masking is such a wild concept. I'm still not sure which is more mind-bending: not knowing you're doing it, or the shock of finally realizing that you are. I didn't know masking was a thing at all—let alone that I'd been doing it for the first 43 years of my life.

That inkling, that sense that I felt better at work, was because of masking. For me, masking has always been a double-edged sword. It's exhausting, but also strangely comforting. In many ways, it felt safer to be at work because I didn't have to *be* me. I could slip into a role, follow a clear script, say the right words at the right time. I knew what was expected: what to wear, how to act, the rules to follow. Even if I didn't consciously realize I was doing it, that act of performing—of hiding behind the role—felt soothing. Predictable. Contained.

At home, none of that existed. There were no scripts, no uniforms, no structured roles to step into. Just me. And I didn't know what to do with that. I didn't know what in the hell I was supposed to say or be. Without a roadmap, I couldn't mask, and without masking, I felt exposed, disoriented, and overwhelmed. It's only now that I understand how common this is for neurodivergent people: we learn to play the part the world expects of us, because it feels safer and more manageable than showing the messy truth of who we are. I excelled at the job itself—the tasks, the checklists, the skills—but I struggled with the relationships, the unspoken dynamics, the invisible social rules that others seemed to just *know*.

In my experience, there are two kinds of masking. One kind is conscious—like deliberately changing how I run to blend in, or laughing at a joke I don't find funny, but I see everyone else is laughing. But there's another kind that's so deeply part of me, I don't even know it's there. It just feels like who I am. But it's not. It's so confusing. Back then, I didn't know any of this, though I did have a vague sense I was two different people. I thought that everyone had a work self and a home self, and that was normal. I didn't really think much about it.

It still seems wild—because even though I know, I can't just turn it off—it just kicks in automatically, like breathing.

After a morning of complete neurodivergent overwhelm and meltdown—hours of screaming, crying, sensory overload, and emotional chaos, I would very simply and seamlessly, without even knowing it, put on my mask as soon as I walked out the front door. With my mask tightly in place, I would complete eight to twelve hours at work. It was like flipping a switch. One moment, I was locked in a trauma spiral with a dysregulated toddler, and the next, I was answering phones, charting notes, smiling politely, moving in and out of patient's rooms, chatting with family members, and saying things like, "No problem at all!" and "Let me check on that for you."

The mask was so much a part of me, I didn't even know it was a mask. I didn't know I was performing. I still sometimes can't even tease out what is a part of my mask and what is really me; it's very confusing. I just knew that at work, there were rules that I knew how to follow. So, I followed them. I wore competence like armor. And no one had any idea that just an hour earlier I had been sobbing on the bathroom floor while my toddler screamed outside the door. They saw someone composed and capable, maybe even impressive.

Holding that mask in place for eight to twelve hours after a full-blown meltdown morning wasn't strength, it was survival. And survival always comes at a cost. Every day, I paid for it with something invisible but essential: my spoons, my internal resources, my energy reserves. These weren't just low, they were depleted. I was running on fumes before the day even began.

That's the nature of burnout—you've already given everything you have, but life keeps demanding more. I didn't know I was in burnout. I don't know how I kept going—how I kept breathing, moving, functioning (albeit barely)—but somehow, I did, kind of.

My memories of that time are so scattered. I wasn't fully present, just limping along, unaware of how much I was struggling. I was trying to rebuild walls, patching large gaping holes with whatever I had—more straw—in a desperate attempt to keep us sheltered, to keep us standing.

Being a single mother and working as a nurse wasn't just depleting. It extracted something from me day after day, until I was hollowed out. I couldn't name what was happening because I didn't have the words or the framework. I didn't know there was a reason I was falling apart. I only knew I was failing at everything that mattered. It cost me my presence. It cost me my ability to respond to Keleigh with patience or warmth, or at all. It cost me the capacity to make dinner, to clean the house, to be the kind of mother I had always imagined I would be. I was being drained of every last drop of clarity, stability, and hope—and I didn't understand why.

When I couldn't meet the demands of the day, my brain and body would shut down completely. I now know these shutdowns are a common neurodivergent response to overwhelm and burnout. My brain literally going offline because it couldn't handle any more. When I was experiencing shutdown and couldn't respond to my child's cries or even keep my eyes open, I wasn't choosing to check out, my nervous system was just overloaded. Even though I'd tell myself I wouldn't do it again, I would, because it wasn't a choice, so I had no control over it.

For me, meltdowns were an explosion of all the emotions and frustrations I didn't know how to process. Screaming, crying, shaking. It was my body's way of trying to release the internal pressure, because there was no other way out. Overwhelm and meltdown are a part of the neurodivergent experience. If I had known that's what I was experiencing, I could have worked on accommodating myself and our life, but I just didn't know or have any reference point.

Looking back on the state of my house, the mess, the disarray, the piles, I can now see multiple layers of neurodivergence at play.

My executive function was virtually nonexistent because I was in full-blown neurodivergent burnout. For me, executive dysfunction is one of the first knobs that gets cranked all the way up when my resources are low.

But there was another layer, too—something I've come to understand more clearly over time, and something I definitely remember experiencing back then.

When I *do* manage to muster some executive function and focus, watch out, world—because I *will* get things done. But my focus becomes so singular that I lose awareness of everything else. That means whatever I touch stays exactly where I touched it. When I did manage to get dressed, every piece of clothing I put on is still out. If I was able to cook something—or even just brought home fast food—everything I used or touched in that process is right where I left it.

It's not about being lazy or messy. It's hard to explain to people who haven't lived it. Folks will say things like, *"Just clean as you go,"* but my brain doesn't register that as part of the task. It's not like I think, *"I should put this away"* and choose not to—I genuinely don't *see* it in that moment. My brain is so narrowly locked onto completing the current task that cleanup doesn't even enter the frame.

So, even when I did manage to do something, anything, it left a visible trail. A mess. Combine this with burnout, and absolutely no support and there was no chance I could have kept my house even remotely tidy.

It's hard to explain how I was clinging to life yet still floating through it looking deceptively normal—dating, wearing nice clothes, doing everyday things like working and shopping. On the surface, I appeared functional and usually looked well put together in a cute outfit. Underneath, I was anything but. I was either crying or dissociating. My inside world didn't match the one on the outside. But no one, including me, had noticed.

I also understand now that my relationship challenges weren't just because I was "bad at dating" (though, let's be honest, sometimes I absolutely was). My difficulties with social connectedness, emotional cues, boundaries, and instinctively understanding people are all traits of my neurodivergence—things I didn't know were part of me. What felt like personal failure was actually a system malfunction. I was running an operating system in a world that never offered me the correct updates.

That lack of intuitive social processing—the thing that let me miss what others might call "obvious"—wasn't subtle. In hindsight, the red flags weren't quiet or sneaky this time around either. They were blaring. Screaming. Fireworks-level warnings. But I didn't register them. I saw something different: kind gestures and loving moments. And when the shift came—when things turned controlling or violent or cruel —I was stunned.

In both cases, with the enraged man and the unhealthy woman, I didn't just *miss* the danger—I rewrote it in real time. I edited their actions into something palatable. Something I could understand. When things spiraled—when the man lashed out and told me I was ruining my child, and when the woman screamed or hit—I was shocked. Genuinely blindsided. Again and again.

Now I understand that undiagnosed neurodivergence doesn't just make *life* confusing, it makes danger confusing. It makes love confusing. It makes abuse confusing. It makes the truth hard to hold, especially when society has taught you to doubt your own perception and assume the best in everyone else.

That is part of the trauma of being undiagnosed. It's not just the confusion—it's the consequences of that confusion. It's the situations you walk into unprotected, unequipped, unaware. It's the deep harm that gets done while you're still just trying to figure out why everything feels so hard.

And so, I walked around like that—half-alive, half-disconnected, and completely confused. Still building with straw. Still trying to make a home from chaos.

The strong narrative I told myself using words like failure, bad mom, lazy, fatally flawed, and shitty human, was all I had. They felt like undeniable truths because I couldn't come up with any other explanation. Now, I know they weren't reflections of who I was, but signs that I was desperately trying to navigate a world built for different brains. Now, I can rewrite the narrative. Instead of "failure," I was overwhelmed. Instead of "lazy," I was in burnout and unable to access my executive function. Instead of "bad mom," I was living in a system that outweighed my abilities at that time. Instead of "fatally flawed," I was wired differently. I was doing the best I could with what I had, even when it didn't feel like enough.

If I had known then what I know now, I could have offered myself so much more compassion. I would have seen that I wasn't a monster or a failure, I was a person whose nervous system was completely overloaded. I would have looked for ways to accommodate my sensory needs, to reduce the demands on my brain, to find help and support instead of trying to carry everything alone. I would have known that I wasn't meant to do it all myself and that wasn't a personal failure.

Now I have the right words—neurodivergent burnout, overwhelm, shutdown, meltdown, alexithymia, executive dysfunction—I finally understand and accept that the person I was during those years wasn't weak, selfish or unfit. She was doing her best with an overwhelmed brain and a heart that loved her child fiercely, even if it didn't always show it in the "right" ways. I can finally hold that version of myself with tenderness, knowing that she was fighting an invisible battle, while still holding space for the trauma we suffered in those years because of it.

I don't know how Keleigh and I survived those years. Looking back, a few things made it possible. Being a nurse meant I wasn't dealing with poverty on top of everything else. I had enough money to get by, and that's a huge privilege. I also benefited from what people call "pretty privilege"—I looked put together enough. Even though getting dressed was its own private battle, I looked competent, and sadly, that matters. These privileges helped me fly under the radar in many ways.

And I had white skin. That alone meant I didn't have to face the layers of systemic racism that would have crushed me entirely. This privilege let me fly under the radar and survive in ways that many Black and Brown neurodivergent mothers are systematically denied.

And then there was Angie. She was Keleigh's stand-in grandma—my ex-girlfriend's mom—and she and her family were the only real support we had. They were the reason we made it through. I'm forever grateful to them; they saved our lives.

Chapter 3: After Collapse, It Gets Better — But Also Worse

I cannot stress enough how much those years nearly cost me my life. I almost gave up, teetering on the edge of something that now I'd call collapse. I wasn't just exhausted—I was at the end of myself. Somehow, at the last possible moment, I rallied. I still don't understand how I pulled myself out. It felt like some kind of miracle, or a glitch in the universe that worked in my favor. Maybe someone up there had my back. Maybe something in me just refused to die.

I still have the list I made on my phone. The title was simple: *I Can Do This*. That list became my lifeline. It held a roadmap of choices I wasn't proud of, but I made them anyway. Quitting my job of six years. Walking away from my house, even though it meant foreclosure. Giving up a cat I loved to the humane society—a decision that still aches, but one I made in a moment of life-or-death urgency. I needed to save myself and Keleigh.

I got rid of nearly everything, and we moved into a tiny apartment near Angie. I left behind furniture, boxes, mail, anything I couldn't carry emotionally or physically. When the bank called, I didn't answer the phone. I stopped opening my mail. I don't even think I filed a change-of-address form. I just… left, walked away and never went back. It was like watching myself in a movie. I didn't know what the hell I was doing. I was hollowed out. But I knew that if I stayed, if I tried to keep playing the part of a person who could manage it all, I wouldn't make it.

That list—those strange, desperate steps that made no logical sense—ended up saving my life. Blind faith and stubborn instinct.

At my new job, I worked alongside Linda, a friend I'd known casually for a while. Slowly, something unexpected began to happen. We started dating and fell in love. In the middle of my unraveling, she became the thread that helped me stitch myself back together. After just a few months together, Linda looked at me one day and said, "We're really fucked up. If we want this to work, we need to go to therapy."

I agreed—not just because I wanted it to work (which I did), but because I didn't know how relationships *were supposed to* work. I didn't have a compass of my own. I hadn't seen healthy modeled. I didn't trust my instincts. So when she said we needed help, I said yes. I was willing to try.

It was during this time, I slowly began to feel better.

Before I could name our experience:

I had an internal monologue telling me it was ridiculous that dating Linda made me feel better. I knew another person couldn't be responsible for my happiness or well-being, so I figured I must be faking it somehow or lying to myself. But I couldn't ignore the fact that when I was around her, I didn't experience extreme emotional volatility or out-of-control reactions. But instead of seeing that as something worth exploring, I took it as more proof that I was failing at life. Clearly, I thought, I *could* be better—so why wasn't I? I didn't spend too much time unpacking it. I assumed this was what life felt like for everyone, and I was handling it worse than most.

I was starting to feel *generally* better, but I still had a lot of underlying struggles. I began making changes I believed I was supposed to make, the kinds of things that were meant to help. I started with clean, healthy eating, which was a huge change. Up to that point, I'd relied almost entirely on ultra-processed and fast food—just eating whatever I could to survive. But now I wanted to be healthier, to be a better mom and partner. I also started going to individual therapy and reading parenting and self-help books, trying to find some kind of roadmap forward.

While I was starting to feel "better," Keleigh's struggles were becoming more and more pronounced. Our life had gone from completely chaotic to *somewhat* more stable. We had moved in with Linda and her three kids, and for the first time, Keleigh had something I never did: a two-parent household where the parents loved each other, spoke kindly, and worked together to build a peaceful home. It felt like a rare gift. I hoped the stability, structure, and healthy practices would ease some of her pain and struggles. But alas, that wasn't the case.

She was around three years old when she first told me she wanted to die—and it wasn't a one-time thing. The suicidal language continued. She was in a near-constant state of heightened distress, always teetering on the edge of an emotional cliff. Everything overwhelmed her. It's hard to describe her in any other way than feral. When school started, things only got worse. In first grade she began bringing home worksheets, and every single attempt to complete one ended in the same way: hours of crying, screaming, bargaining, bribing, and begging, and still incomplete worksheets to school the following day. Nothing was ever simple (and that's putting it pretty mildly).

Sleep offered no relief. Even on the rare nights when Keleigh managed to rest, she was tormented by nightmares and night terrors. I'd hear her crying in her sleep, or relentlessly grinding her teeth, or she'd wake up screaming, trembling, terrified. She never had a moment of complete calm.

Her frustration tolerance was nonexistent. Her words were often shocking—saying she wanted to die, or that she wanted to kill me, or worse: that she wanted me to *watch* her die. She'd slam her head against the wall, bite herself, hit me. I didn't know what was happening.

We saw Keleigh as a child shaped by trauma, but also as explosive, manipulative, disruptive, and sometimes even harmful or abusive. The lens we were using back then framed her behavior as intentional. We told ourselves things like: *"She's just being dramatic," "She's throwing a tantrum for attention," "She needs stricter discipline," "She's manipulating us with her emotions," "She freaks out over nothing."*

We saw her actions as choices—as things she *could* control if we just found the right parenting strategy. We tried everything. Punishments. Rewards. Visual schedules. Heart-to-hearts. Behavior charts. Calming corners. Consequences. Conversations. The list goes on and on.

Nothing helped—in fact, most of it made things worse. She didn't calm down. She escalated. We escalated. Our straw house would catch fire, and I'd try to put it out by blowing on it.

When she was very young, I started taking her to therapy, desperate for help. But it was never even remotely successful. Time after time, we were dismissed—sometimes literally—because providers didn't see a problem. I tried to explain, tried to put words to what we were living through, but no one really listened. On the surface, we looked fine. She was meeting milestones, staying afloat. From the outside, she seemed to be functional enough.

One provider told me I just needed to "stipulate her non-stop" —even suggesting I threaten to withhold food until she complied. I had already tried structured, consequence-based approaches (not to that extreme), and they didn't work for her, or for me. That advice wasn't just unhelpful, it was dangerous. Another therapist actually recommended using physical intimidation, scaring Keleigh into compliance. Needless to say, we didn't go back.

Keleigh's "behavior" was a daily battle. Linda and I agreed on nearly everything else in life, but when it came to parenting Keleigh, we often found ourselves at odds. It wasn't that we were constantly arguing, but it was an ongoing conversation—our one persistent source of tension. I sometimes felt like I could relate to Keleigh on a deep, unspoken level, and that made it seem like Linda just didn't understand her in the same way. But the truth is, I didn't fully understand her either. I only knew what didn't help. I had no idea what actually would help.

Linda always felt strongly about how Keleigh treated me. Linda was fiercely protective of me and didn't think it was right for Keleigh to speak to me in such hurtful ways. When Keleigh yelled or lashed out, Linda often stepped in, responding in a "typical" parental way—setting boundaries, trying to hold the line. Sometimes I would agree, or try to agree, for lack of knowing what else to do or think, but it never really worked out.

In my mind, it was all my fault. Everything Keleigh was struggling with could be traced back to our shared trauma. I believed that because I had failed her so deeply, it wasn't right to punish her for having a response to that. Punishment never helped anyway—it only escalated her, escalated me, and pulled everything further out of control.

I had a vague sense that Keleigh wasn't able to control her outbursts. I couldn't fully explain it, but I would say things like, "I think I know what it's like to feel like her," or "I think I used to feel like that as a kid." But I didn't really know. I just assumed everyone must have moments like that or sometimes feel that way. I believed that with enough stability, love, and guidance, she'd eventually "get over" these "behaviors."

This was all compounded by a strange, recurring pattern that Linda and I didn't understand. Linda would bring up something I had said or done—or something Keleigh had said or done—and I would have absolutely no memory of it. Not even a flicker. This happened so often that, over the years, it became its own source of tension. From my perspective, it felt like Linda must be exaggerating or misremembering. From

Linda's, it seemed like I was gaslighting her—denying things that had just happened, as if I was trying to manipulate or deflect. It was extremely confusing.

On the work front, I was starting to feel unsettled. Every job felt like the wrong fit, like something wasn't clicking. At my previous job, I had worked closely with my boss and truly believed we made a great team. We took breaks together, shared stories, I bought her breakfast and we'd eat together in the morning and every day before I left, I'd ask if she needed anything else from me. I genuinely liked her and thought of her as both a good friend and a supportive coworker.

At some point, I asked if I could list her as a reference. She agreed, and I started applying for new positions, listing her name each time. I had great interviews but kept hitting dead ends—no callbacks, no offers. Nursing is a competitive field, so at first, I chalked it up to bad luck.

Eventually, I started to miss the familiarity of my old job and tried to go back, but I couldn't get a return call. Then another nurse told me something shocking: she had asked my old boss—my "friend"—if they'd consider bringing me back, and my boss told her she'd *never* rehire me. That alone stung, but it got worse. I also found out she had been sabotaging my job interviews.

It was that strange, familiar confusion—the feeling that I knew someone, or understood our relationship, only to suddenly hit a wall where, out of nowhere, they seemed to change. This example left me bewildered. It felt so bizarre, and I couldn't make any sense of it at all.

The straw house I had been trying to rebuild was finally starting to feel a little sturdier. The walls weren't strong, but they were standing. I wasn't thriving, but I wasn't collapsing either. I had patched everything together with whatever I could find—routine, therapy, clean eating, Linda's love. Keleigh's part of the house, though, was in bad shape. No matter how carefully I tried to reinforce the walls, it just kept caving in. It was creaking, cracking, and swaying beside me, and I had no idea how to fix it. All I knew was that the storm was not letting up.

Now that I have the right words:

Looking back, I can see that all those drastic changes I made—quitting my job, walking away from my house, cutting ties with everything that felt too heavy—were just ways of lowering my daily demands so I could move out of burnout. I wasn't consciously making accommodations. But in the late-diagnosed world, we often call those *accidental accommodations*—the unintentional shifts we make just to stay alive, not realizing we're building the scaffolding we actually need.

What I didn't know was that my brain wasn't broken, it was just neurodivergent. One of the most fundamental challenges for neurodivergent brains, especially those with ADHD, is dopamine. We don't have the same steady supply or delivery system as neurotypical brains. I think of it like this: in a neurotypical brain, dopamine follows a clear, well-marked path. In my brain, there are multiple paths. It's over stimulating and chaotic, and dopamine often gets lost or stuck in traffic. It doesn't travel efficiently, so motivation, focus, reward—none of them work the way they're "supposed" to.

Which is fine, except the entire world is built for people whose dopamine arrives on time and in order.

Falling in love with Linda gave my dopamine-starved brain the jolt it desperately needed. Without knowing it, that relationship became a turning point—one of the first steps in pulling me out of my burnout. In the years leading up to it, when I had some awareness that I was struggling, I always thought I was just stressed or depressed. I did what we're told to do when we feel that way: I pushed myself to socialize more. I went to bars, surrounded myself with loud music, flashing lights, and noisy conversations. It felt like the prescribed antidote to sadness or isolation, and I thought it would help.

But when I started dating Linda, everything shifted. Our time together was quiet. We had backyard campfires, kids' movie nights, slow dinners without blaring TVs or crowded rooms. It wasn't just her presence—it was the peace. The quiet. The steady removal of sensory chaos. I didn't understand it at the time, but it was exactly what my brain had been craving. For the first time, my nervous system could exhale. There was space to think, to feel, to just *be*—without completely drowning in overwhelm.

Linda was different from anyone I'd been with before. She seemed to recognize my vulnerabilities—maybe not consciously, maybe not all the way—but enough to instinctively protect me. And to this day, she still does. For the first time in an intimate relationship, I felt truly safe and secure. That safety had a profound impact on my nervous system. It was as if my body received a particular signal for the first time: *you can rest now.*

She made it safe enough for me to begin healing.

For a long time, I beat myself up for "needing" Linda to feel better. I saw it as a weakness—proof that I was broken or too dependent. But now I understand it differently. It wasn't just about needing a person. It was about what we created together. The love, the safety, the *environment* we built. That was what finally gave my nervous system the room it had always needed. A space that didn't constantly drain me or rob my soul of its last ounce of life.

There's no clear line where burnout ends. It's more like overlapping phases, where the worst of it slowly fades and you start to find moments of stability. But even as I got better, many of my struggles didn't go away. They just looked different.

As I got better at surviving day-to-day, I also got better at masking. Without realizing it, I doubled down on hiding my struggles—both from Linda and from myself.

Now that I can reflect back through a new lens, I understand why Linda and I seemed to align on everything—except when it came to Keleigh. We agreed on nearly everything else: our worldviews, our morals, our daily routines. I used to say, "We're like the same person!", and I believed that. But now I know that I was unconsciously mirroring her—adopting her preferences, her tone, even her ways of thinking—without realizing I was doing it.

Being undiagnosed meant I didn't know I was operating with a completely different system—one that didn't naturally interpret or respond to the world in the same way. Instead, I had learned to mimic others as a way to survive and belong.

This kind of mirroring is very common in autistic people, especially those socialized as girls or women. We become experts at picking up on subtle cues and adapting our behavior to match what we think is expected of us. We absorb the preferences, habits, and even the language of the people around us—not out of manipulation, but as a kind of unconscious survival instinct: *If I can act like you, maybe I'll be okay here.*

Over time, this mirroring can become so automatic, so deeply ingrained, that it's hard to tell where the mask ends and the real self begins. That's why I didn't recognize how much I was borrowing Linda's way of being—it felt real, because in those moments, it was, and still is.

That strange, unexplainable pattern between Linda and me, where I could never seem to recall things she said had just happened. It was incredibly confusing and created a lot of tension between us. But now I understand it clearly: I was experiencing a neurodivergent threat response—specifically, shutdown and dissociation.

My brain was so overloaded by demands, emotional tension, and confusion that it would go into freeze mode. I was experiencing something called functional freeze. I looked physically present and even carried on conversations, but mentally, I wasn't there. My brain wasn't recording anything. I wasn't forming memories because I was dissociating—checking out completely in order to survive the overwhelm.

Now I understand this, I can let go of my worry that I was accidentally manipulating Linda, or somehow tricking her on purpose. For years I asked Google things like, *"Can you gaslight someone by accident?"* because I was just so confused. But I see now that this wasn't manipulation. It wasn't gaslighting. It was my brain's involuntary response to constant sensory, emotional, and cognitive overload.

On top of that, I was living with intense Rejection Sensitive Dysphoria (RSD)—a neurodivergent trait that can turn even small misunderstandings or gentle suggestions into personal catastrophes. Every disagreement or even potential disagreement felt like an existential threat. When Linda would innocently point something out—no matter how minor—it felt so threatening to my nervous system that I would instantly shift into a severe threat response. I'd freeze, shut down, and dissociate almost automatically.

The dynamic was painful for both of us. Linda saw me as minimizing or dodging responsibility. I saw myself as broken, or bad, but it was just my nervous system doing its best to protect me, using the only tools it had.

Seeing this now—with the right words and framework—gives me so much compassion for both of us. My dissociation wasn't personal. It wasn't malicious. It was a survival strategy, hardwired into a brain and body that had spent too many years in crisis.

Looking back on Keleigh's struggles, I know that her intense meltdowns, violent outbursts, and even the shocking things she said weren't signs that she was "bad" or "defiant." They were the result of neurodivergent overwhelm, meltdown, and threat responses. What we used to see as "behaviors" or "choices" were actually her brain and nervous system reacting to a world that felt constantly unsafe.

Back then, I didn't know what a threat response was, but now, with my newfound language and understanding, it's clear how deeply Keleigh was impacted by PDA (Pathological Demand Avoidance). Sometimes called Persistent Drive for Autonomy, PDA is a profile of neurodivergence characterized by a baseline level of nervous system dysregulation and/or elevation. Because the system is already running hot, even the smallest demands can register as threats. A demand might be something as simple as brushing teeth, using the bathroom, or even having someone else ask you a question, because at its core, even a question is a demand for a response. The system can also be easily overwhelmed by someone having any authority over them or even the tiniest threat to their own autonomy. This isn't about opposition or rebellion or manipulation, it's about a nervous system that interprets everyday life as dangerous.

When a demand or threat to autonomy triggers a threat response in an already dysregulated system, the next phase is often equalizing. This is the nervous system's attempt to bring the perceived threat down to its level, or ideally, below it. Equalizing can happen internally or externally, but it often appears completely disproportionate to the situation. It might include threats of violence, self-harm, screaming, breaking things, or total shutdown. The body has entered a life-or-death panic. The prefrontal cortex is offline, and the reptilian brain—the oldest part of the brain, responsible for survival—is in full control. It often looks and feels very immature, because that immature part of our brains is in the driver's seat. To someone outside the experience, it can look like rage or manipulation. But to the person experiencing it, without even knowing it, equalizing is about survival—it's the nervous system doing whatever it takes to feel less powerless.

The hardest part of all this? It's entirely subconscious. There's not a single part of this process that involves conscious choice or deliberate thinking. When we don't understand PDA, —nor have the language to explain it—it's so easy to believe we're fundamentally wrong or fatally flawed. We're left with questions like: *Why am I so mean? What's wrong with me? Why am I such a bitch?* But these aren't moral failings or personality flaws—they're the body's desperate, instinctive fight to feel safe.

For Keleigh, equalizing often looked like threatening to harm herself—or us—over the smallest everyday expectations. A simple ask like "please put on your shoes" could send her into a spiral. She might scream that she wanted to die, or that she would kill me, or that we should all die together. It was terrifying and heartbreaking. As she got older, and the demands of life naturally increased, so did the intensity of her responses. At the time, we thought she was out of control, but she was simply trying to survive.

It wasn't that she didn't want to do something—it was that any expectation, even the smallest one, felt like a life-threatening demand to her brain. When you're constantly feeling under threat, everything becomes a trigger. Traditional parenting approaches didn't help because those approaches are built on the idea that the child has control and is making choices. Keleigh wasn't making choices. She was responding to her body's alarms.

Her over-the-top responses weren't deliberate defiance or manipulation—they were meltdowns and threat responses. The biting, the hitting, the desperate words—these were all ways her overwhelmed system was trying to protect itself. The more we tried to force, control, or fix it, the more she escalated, because she felt so trapped.

Now I understand that it was never about her not trying hard enough, or me not being a good enough parent, or Linda not understanding. It was about Keleigh experiencing the world in a way that neither of us fully understood—an experience of constant overwhelm where even the gentlest expectation felt unbearable. She needed safety and co-regulation; no punishment or reward would ever help.

All of this was compounded by Keleigh experiencing Rejection Sensitive Dysphoria (RSD). It wasn't just demands that felt threatening—it was the fear of failing or disappointing, or any perceived rejection that made the stakes feel unbearable. Her brain and body weren't reacting to expectations; they were reacting to shame, panic, and an intense fear of disconnection. Where my reaction to RSD was freeze, Keleigh's was almost always fight.

We were two neurodivergent souls caught in a storm while living in a straw house. We had no words, no understanding, no weather report, and no safe space. But at least now, I finally have the right words, and with them, a blueprint for how to hold our pain with compassion instead of shame. Back then, I couldn't give us safety. But now, I can name what we needed—and begin its construction.

Chapter 4: Keleigh's Room Keeps Collapsing

Before I could name our experience:

I kept moving through life, collecting healing practices and throwing myself into them completely. I did everything—yoga, meditation, journaling, therapy, forest bathing, healthy eating, hiking, even laying naked on the earth, begging the universe for answers.

Emotionally, I felt better *and* not better. The healing tools did bring some surface calm to my nervous system, but underneath, I was still struggling. I wrestled with frequent irritation over small things, mood swings that felt like emotional whiplash, and crying—so much crying. I often wondered if I was emotionally immature—if something was so fundamentally wrong with me, all the healing in the world couldn't fix it.

There was always a quiet hum of confusion in the background, like unstoppable static. But there was also something I didn't realize other people *never* experienced. So, I didn't ask about it—how could I, without the words or any idea that it was unusual? It was just this ever-present sense that no matter how hard I tried, I couldn't quite *land*. I kept telling myself that if I could just find one more practice, one more solution, I'd finally feel clear, grounded, better. That longing drove me —frantically, obsessively. And because I believed that was true for me, I believed it had to be true for Keleigh too. If I could just find the thing, we could both finally be okay.

At the time, I held a deeply rooted belief that everything we were experiencing was trauma-based. And it made sense— Keleigh and I had both lived through more than our fair share, even her entrance into the world had been traumatic.

So I poured everything I had into the pursuit of healing—for both of us. It became my full-time job. Healing us was all I thought about. It consumed me.

I clung to journaling. Looking back at those entries now is devastating. I wrote the same lines over and over again, trying to convince myself they were true: *"I want to be a good mom. I love Keleigh. I love the other kids."* (I'd write each of their names back then, but I'm simplifying here for you, the reader.) These lines became mantras—words I hoped would eventually sink in. I filled pages with phrases I wanted to remember, things I'd picked up from books or online articles— scripts I thought "good moms" were supposed to say. During journaling sessions, I would practice saying them out loud.

Other journal entries revealed even more despair. One has a list entitled *"Things to help us"* the list includes all kinds of things I'd already been doing therapy, hiking, hypnotherapy, etc. in between items I had written *"I don't know,"* "these are *dumb and won't help,"* and *"truly I don't know."* I knew I had already committed to these practices, without any success at all, so it felt pointless.

One entry dated from 2018 says *"Today was hard. I feel like my whole life I've never really known what to do, what I should do, or even what I want to do. Today I feel like I was pretty honest with myself. I have a stress problem or a stress management problem, or some kind of problem and I've passed it on to Keleigh genetically or environmentally, either way, it is horrible. I wish I knew how to fix it. I am trying to be hopeful about some new options I'm exploring, but it is hard to continue to remain hopeful as I feel just buried by this burden. I can remember having some outbursts as a child and in my 20's, but I know they got really bad when I had Keleigh and went through my really hard times, so I guess it's stress management problem of sorts. I want to help Keleigh find ways to find some peace in her soul. This week has been really hard…I always tell myself all I can do is keep moving forward, but I don't know if that's good enough anymore…"*

In 2019, more similar entries, *"I wish I could respond the way I want to respond. I know that's how she (Keleigh) must feel too. I feel like a failure, like I'm never going to get it right. I don't know what to do to help her, but I feel like I must help myself first. I'm going to have to figure it out, but I don't know how to do it."*

I was obsessed with trying to help Keleigh. I believed everything stemmed from trauma, and I blamed myself entirely.

I devoured self-help and parenting books, trying every strategy they suggested—behavior charts, reward systems, consequence-based discipline, therapy, nature walks, yoga for kids, even hypnotherapy. We spent endless hours in the forest. Nothing helped. The only things that brought Keleigh even a sliver of relief were getting enough sleep (a challenge in and of itself) and, surprisingly, loud rap music. But even that didn't come until she was around twelve. Everything else only seemed to make things worse.

As time went on, a growing rift came between Linda and me. We both loved Keleigh deeply and wanted what was best for her, but we didn't always agree on how to help. It became an ongoing conversation—because it was always on my mind. And the more we talked about it, the more tension it created. What started as concern often turned into disagreement, and sometimes, contention.

At this time, something else started to come up between Linda and I. She began telling me that I wasn't connecting with her. At first, I was confused. I was connecting. I showed up for her every day. I loved her deeply. And because I loved her so much, I couldn't believe she didn't feel it. I was gutted. If the person I loved more than anyone couldn't feel that love, what did that say about me? I felt like a failure again, in the one area that mattered most.

I didn't understand what she meant when she said I felt distant and surface-level. I thought I was being present. I thought I was doing everything "right."

But it kept coming up. Again and again, she would say that she felt like something was missing, that I wasn't really with her. That I was giving her words, but not feelings. That she didn't know what was going on inside me because I wasn't letting her in. And that confused me even more, because I genuinely didn't know what she meant by "letting her in." I wasn't keeping anything out. I just didn't know what else there was to give.

So, in typical fashion, I tried to fix it.

I started googling phrases like "how to emotionally connect with your partner," "how to be more vulnerable in a relationship," and "what to say to help someone feel close to you." I read everything I could find. I studied emotional intimacy like it was a foreign language.

I memorized sentences that seemed meaningful and tried to use them in conversations. I thought if I could say the right things—if I could mimic the language of emotional closeness—then she'd feel it, and everything would be okay. But no matter what I said, she still felt that I wasn't really there. That I wasn't letting her see me.

It was maddening.

I got serious. I made emotional connection my new project. I journaled every single day for over a year and a half, using an emotion wheel to track my feelings. I didn't just dabble, I committed. I read books. I watched videos. I listened to podcasts. I tried every practice I could find; mirror work, inner child letters, shadow work, guided meditations, self-inquiry exercises, writing letters to myself and burning them. I was determined to crack the code.

At one point, I was working with a holistic practitioner. She told me I was likely hiding my emotions, burying them out of fear of how others might respond, and that I simply needed to let that go, and just say how I was feeling. So I dug deeper. I tried to excavate whatever was buried. I assumed there was a well of emotion inside me—I just didn't know how to access it yet.

Keleigh continued to struggle, both at school and socially. Her "behaviors" were relentless. There were no breaks for any of us. Daily life was utterly exhausting.

Getting ready for the day remained a nightmare. I'd wake up hours early, trying to prepare myself with yoga, meditation, affirmations, baths, lists, schedules, plans, everything. But no matter what I did, nearly every morning ended in chaos and tears. Keleigh would go to school crying, and I'd head to work the same way. We'd both push through the day, just trying to survive.

By middle school, Keleigh's suffering only intensified. Everything felt like a trigger, and her reactions were explosive. I always responded with the best of intentions, but it often made things worse. The escalation would spiral until she'd beg us to give her up for adoption, leave her behind, or take her to a psych hospital. I'd break down at the things she was saying, crying, and pleading with her to stop, desperately trying to reason with her. It almost always ended with both of us in full-blown distress—panic, shaking, sobbing—completely overwhelmed.

She had started cutting herself, and her body was covered in marks. One morning during the drive to school, I was desperately rattling off every possible solution I could think of —therapy, nature walks, anything. She screamed at me that she didn't want any of it. That she hated all of it. That none of it helped, and that she would refuse to go if I tried to make her do any of them. I said something like, "But it can't feel good to always feel this way."

She looked at me—her face tight with tension, heavy with disdain for life, and hollow in that familiar, dead-inside way, the only expression I'd seen on her face since the day she was born and said, "Mom, I've *never* felt good."

And she was right. She had lived thirteen years in this body, in this world, and had never once felt good in her own skin. It broke me. I felt the weight of her words like the world had just been dropped onto my shoulders. A deep, desperate urgency rushed through me—a need to undo her pain and fix what felt so impossibly broken. I still believed it was all my fault. Grief, guilt, and helplessness crashed into me.

Until that point, I had tried everything apart from traditional psychiatry and medication. Both Linda and I worked in the behavior health field, so we had a behind-the-scenes understanding of the system. I've always had complicated feelings about healthcare, especially when it comes to psychiatry, and I had not wanted to pursue that path up to this point.

But in a moment of raw desperation, I started researching IV ketamine. It was a drastic move, but something in me pushed forward. I found a provider in New Hampshire who was willing to treat a thirteen-year-old.

We drove there, and Keleigh received six IV ketamine treatments. The providers kept asking when she'd last felt good, and we kept giving the same answer: "Never." Her depression scores were the maximum score possible. The provider was alarmed and started her on a high dose of Paxil alongside large doses of IV ketamine.

The Paxil had disastrous effects. It was way too much, far too fast. My nurse brain was screaming that it wasn't right, but the provider was adamant. She told me that if we didn't act fast, Keleigh might not survive. She made it sound like this was the only option, and I was desperate, even though everything in me was questioning it.

It backfired. Hard. We were all carrying the weight of thirteen years of confusion and desperation, trying to survive something we couldn't accurately describe. The constant crises had worn all three of us down. And for me I still had this weird fog and confusion around me, but also didn't really know it or have a name for it.

Keleigh couldn't be left alone for even a second because she was a danger to herself and others. Linda and I had to sleep on the floor with her, with one of us on either side. It was the worst kind of nightmare, like her already over activated system had somehow found a whole new level of chaos. We weren't prepared, but we were lucky. We had experience and training, and we used every bit of it to keep her safe at home.

At first, we thought it was the ketamine. We thought *what the hell have we done*? But within a week or two, I realized—it wasn't the ketamine. It was the Paxil. The dose had been way too high, and the provider had moved way too fast. My nurse instincts had known better, but I'd been desperate enough to override them. Once I tapered her off the medication, she gradually returned to her "normal"—which still meant constant dysregulation. But at least it was familiar and we knew how to survive it.

But that small relief—returning to her "normal" state of dysregulation—was short-lived. Not long after, Keleigh threatened to shoot someone at school. Rightfully, alarms were raised. But for me, the desperation only deepened. The weight I had been carrying on my shoulders—the weight of our entire world—suddenly felt like the weight of the universe. I felt like a cornered, rabid animal—completely flooded, out of options, and barely surviving under the pressure. To say I was desperate is a wild understatement.

Around this time, Keleigh started telling me she thought she had ADHD. She said it more than once, but I kept brushing it off, convinced it was the trauma, and that it was all my fault. I kept telling her she didn't have ADHD. I was terrified she'd get a label for something I had caused.

Thanks to reading no less than one thousand parenting and self-help books, I had stumbled across a book by Dr. Daniel Amen. It outlined his approach to psychiatry, and something about it clicked for me. There are all kinds of opinions out there about The Amen Clinics, and I will let you form your own; however, it is a major part of our story, and I do credit them with saving my daughter's life.

The Amen Clinics' approach to psychiatric care stood out to me for several reasons—all of which I found compelling, especially from my perspective as a healthcare professional. First, it's a cash-based model, which automatically means a different kind of patient-provider relationship and often a more tailored approach. (I feel horrible saying that, but I've found it to be true). Second, their intake process is incredibly thorough—more comprehensive than anything I'd seen in standard care. Finally, and most importantly, they use something called a SPECT scan: a functional brain imaging tool, that allows them to actually *see* what's happening in the brain. Dr. Amen's core belief is that psychiatry is the only field of medicine that doesn't look at the organ it treats—and so his clinics do just that.

The idea of seeing the brain—and treating it based on what's physically happening rather than just what someone says out loud—made sense to me in a way most psychiatric models never had. And for me, when something makes sense, it tends to stick. If something doesn't feel like a good fit, I can't force myself to do it. Which, admittedly, has caused some problems over the course of my life.

But I digress.

I wanted to take Keleigh to the clinic, but Linda was hesitant. She felt that Keleigh's fragile system needed time to rest after the horrible side effects of the Paxil. She wanted to give her space to recover before we jumped into the next thing. But as is somewhat typical between us, I ignored her hesitation, made the appointment, and we went to D.C.

No matter how many healing practices I stacked up like straw bales, no matter how fiercely I tried to patch the cracks or brace the beams, Keleigh's part of the house just wouldn't hold. I kept rebuilding, reimagining, and reinforcing, but her room kept collapsing—and it wasn't through lack of love or effort. I was working with everything I had, and then some, but the truth was, I didn't understand the architecture. I was using the wrong materials for a structure I couldn't clearly see. And so, despite all my desperate repairs, the walls kept caving in, over and over again.

Now that I have the words:

Now I can see how much I misunderstood what was happening inside me. Back then, I believed I was on a healing journey—and in some ways, I was. I believe I did heal from a lot of the trauma I had experienced. But at the same time, many of the "healthy" tools I gathered (though valuable in their own right) taught me to dismiss my own reality. In hindsight, they often became tools for masking—ways to appear well, even when I wasn't. I convinced myself I was getting better simply because I had learned to pretend I wasn't struggling.

The practices gave me moments of calm, but they also fed the illusion that if I just tried harder—just added one more thing—I could finally fix myself. I didn't yet understand what was really happening, so I clung to mantras and memorized scripts, hoping to transform myself into someone who didn't feel my feelings every single day.

The practicing scripts? Another neurodivergent thing I was doing without knowing it was a neurodivergent thing. I would rehearse scripts, conversations, and scenarios in my head, sometimes dozens of times, trying to get the words just right. I wasn't being fake. I was trying to compensate for something I couldn't name at the time: an absence of intuitive social processing. I never just *knew* what to say the way others seemed to. So if I wanted to get it right—or even close—I had to practice.

The other journal entries highlight the pain and confusion that comes with an undiagnosed or a misdiagnosis.

Looking back, I can see that Linda's early sense that I wasn't connecting with her was actually our first real clue. At the time, it felt like such a painful failing—like I was somehow withholding something or just doing it wrong. But now we understand that alexithymia was at play. She was trying to connect with me in the ways *she* feels connection—through shared emotion, expressed vulnerability, mutual resonance, but my brain just doesn't work like that. I wasn't keeping her out. I was simply wired differently. Without the right language for it, though, it felt like a breakdown. Like I was emotionally broken. Like I was failing at love.

Parenting a disabled or neurodivergent child—especially without the right words, support, or framework—can wear down even the most deeply connected parents. The chronic stress, the constant emotional upheaval, the sheer number of decisions that must be made each day—it all takes its toll. Even when both people love the child, and love each other, the pressure can strain every part of their relationship.

In our case, I was unknowingly bringing my own neurodivergence into the mix. I wasn't just a mother trying to support my neurodivergent child—I was an undiagnosed neurodivergent adult, unsupported, and completely unaware of how my own brain functioned. I was living with executive dysfunction, emotional dysregulation, rejection sensitive dysphoria, PDA threat responses, alexithymia, bottom-up thinking, and a host of other invisible barriers.

I was also trying to work and maintain a household with the other children, while pouring everything I had into helping Keleigh. It's no wonder tensions rose. Linda and I weren't just overwhelmed—we were operating blind, using the wrong tools, and following a different set of directions. Looking back, it's clear we had virtually no chance of successfully navigating everything.

Keleigh wasn't "just traumatized", "too sensitive" or "acting out for attention." She was neurodivergent and completely misunderstood. She wasn't broken, bad, dramatic, or manipulative. Her brain was wired differently, and nearly every system in her life—home, school, society, even me—was demanding that she function in impossible ways.

Keleigh's nervous system was on constant high alert. What looked like defiance was a threat response. What looked like volatility was sensory overload. What looked like laziness was executive dysfunction. What looked like neediness was a deep pattern of shared co-dysregulation.

She has PDA, but the demand avoidance wasn't oppositional, it was instinctual. She had rejection sensitivity that made even neutral feedback feel like proof she was unlovable. Her brain simply didn't sort information, emotion, or communication in the same way as other people's brains. The chaos wasn't *hers*, but chaos ensued when we all used neurotypical tools and lens.

By the time Keleigh was thirteen, she wasn't just dysregulated; she was in a full-blown state of neurodivergent burnout. Her system had spent years masking, coping, compensating, and failing to be understood. Every attempt to help her added to the pressure because they didn't match her neurology. Every moment of being misread, mislabeled, or misunderstood chipped away at her capacity.

Burnout wasn't the cause of her struggles—it was the *accumulation* of them. It was the end result of being unsupported in all the ways that mattered. Her system had been running on survival mode for thirteen years straight, and so it was breaking down. Her collapse was understandable—once we finally looked through the right lens.

Ketamine wasn't a good choice for Keleigh. It's often used to treat severe depression by building or strengthening under active brain pathways. But for someone like Keleigh—whose neurodivergent brain was already flooded with overactivity—it didn't make sense.

Even though her depression markers were off the charts, it's a clear example of how, in psychiatry, many boxes can be checked at once. Symptoms can overlap across conditions, and without the right framework, it's easy to misread what's really happening beneath the surface.

That's not to say ketamine is a bad treatment—it just wasn't right for Keleigh. So many psychiatric approaches are built around neurotypical models, and when you try to apply those models to a brain that's wired differently, they often miss the mark.

One last note about that inkling I had—that the Amen Clinic might be a good fit. That might sound minor, but over the years, this small concept has caused me quite a bit of grief.

Historically, when something doesn't quite add up—even just one small detail—I hit a wall. My brain goes into lockdown mode. I can't fake agreement or compliance. I *have* faked it before, but when I'm forcing myself to do something that doesn't align, it isn't pretty. Not only is it usually obvious that I'm faking, but I'm also not pleasant when I'm pushing through something. I've always hated this about myself—because it seems like I should just be able to do the damn thing. Sometimes I *want* to just do the damn thing.

My system can't override misalignment. I usually end up crumbling, crying, or becoming extremely irritable. It often just looked like I was being rigid, or like I was just being a bitch. But I wasn't trying to be difficult. I just didn't have the language for what I was experiencing internally.

The way my brain works is likely tied to something called *bottom-up processing.* Bottom-up thinkers tend to process the world by starting with the details: sensory input, concrete information, lived experience—and then building toward a bigger picture. We don't begin with broad concepts or abstract frameworks. Our understanding comes from collecting all the little pieces and sensing how they fit together.

When something genuinely makes sense—when all the pieces align—my brain gives a full-body *yes*. I can move forward with clarity and energy, even excitement.

That's why, when the Amen Clinic made sense to me, I didn't hesitate—I ignored Linda's caution and just went for it.

Our straw house was kind of standing, but parts of it had collapsed. This wasn't surprising—after all, it was a house built long ago by my family, my ancestors, and my past. They did the best they could with the tools and knowledge they had, just as I had. But soon—finally—we would uncover something that had never been part of the original design: a foundation strong enough to hold us. Not an old blueprint rediscovered, not more straw, but a new understanding born from everything we had endured. What came next would allow us to rebuild—not from fear, but from truth. No longer would our shelter be made from straw, but something more solid.

Chapter 5: Things Finally Start to ADD Up

Loud, gritty, profane, at times insanely clever, and occasionally absurdly sweet: rap music. This is where our life intersects with the one and only thing I've ever found that truly calms Keleigh's soul. Rap, Hip Hop, and R&B. The lyrics weren't always exactly what I'd call appropriate for young listeners, but it didn't matter.

I discovered the connection by accident. We were driving, and some kind of radio-friendly rap song came on the radio. Keleigh rolled her window down and closed her eyes. She started gently and intuitively moving her body to the rhythm. Then she began to sing along. I was stunned. I had never seen her system relax like that. Her shoulders were loose, her body soft, her face free of tension. No crying. No screaming. No flailing. Just peace. It was unbelievable.

At first, I thought it was a fluke. But the next day, I tried it again—this time on purpose. And it worked. She began asking to go for rides around town so we could blast "our" rap music. The radio versions weren't enough; we needed the real deal. She loved it. She wasn't just tolerating the world in those moments—she was connected to something bigger, something that met her exactly where she was. Perhaps it didn't ask her to be calmer. Perhaps the beat somehow speaks to her soul. I don't know the reason, but I know it works. We would ride around for hours while she sang and moved and let the wind tangle her hair. For the first time in her life, she had some sort of peace.

Who would've guessed rap music was the key? After years of sneaking in meditations, forest bathing, therapy, and whispering affirmations into the wind, *rap* was the thing that finally brought Keleigh's nervous system to a tolerable place. I certainly didn't see it coming, but I have never been more grateful to any other art form or genre of music.

So, Nikki Minaj, Lil Wayne, and some old school 50 Cent on blast as we hit the highway to the Amen Clinic. I had a flicker of hope—and I tend to have very high expectations, especially around mental health care. I didn't want to get my hopes up, but I couldn't help it. Something about this felt different.

Keleigh, on the other hand, was *not* feeling it, and that's putting it mildly. She rolled her eyes through nearly every moment of the process. She cried. She struggled. She wanted to go home. The long intake and assessment process felt endless to her, and it *was* a lot—questionnaires, interviews, scans. She didn't believe it, or anything, would help.

Keleigh felt broken. She couldn't understand why we were putting so much energy into something she was sure would fail, like everything else had. Her hopelessness was deep, raw, and real.

Finally, the day arrives. We meet the child psychiatrist at the Amen Clinic who will reveal the results of Keleigh's brain scan and take over her treatment and care. He dives right in, pulling up Keleigh's brain scans on the screen. Within minutes, we're looking at images of her brain at rest and during concentration. And what we see is shocking.

He points to the areas that aren't functioning the way they should—regions that are either under active, overactive, or lighting up in places that don't make sense. The images are intense and undeniable.

And then he says it.

"These results are consistent with ADHD."

The doctor gave her two additional diagnoses.

The first was Disruptive Mood Dysregulation Disorder—DMDD. He explained that it's a diagnosis often used in cases of Autism, and while he wasn't labeling her as autistic (this isn't something they do there), the overlap was clear. Her mood dysregulation wasn't a behavioral issue—it was neurological.

The third diagnosis, I saw coming. But still, when he said it, my heart sank.

PTSD.

He pointed to the patterns in her brain, the unmistakable signs of trauma. As he spoke, I started to cry. I felt so awful about everything she'd lived through. Everything I couldn't protect her from. Everything I hadn't understood.

Even though I had suspected it, seeing it confirmed visually, medically, and scientifically hit me like a tidal wave.

When I heard the words ADHD, I did what I always do—I dove in headfirst and became completely obsessed with learning everything I could. It wasn't just curiosity. It was survival. I needed to understand what this meant for Keleigh and what we were dealing with.

ADHD isn't just about attention and hyperactivity. It's what the name implies, but there are so many other facets. I had done some training and education in the past around Alzheimer's and dementia, and something from that training came flooding back: when the wiring of the brain is impacted, it's never just *one* thing that's affected—it's everything. The brain is responsible for everything! When our brain is impacted, so is every thought, feeling, action, and moment.

As I started reading about ADHD, not the surface-level stuff, but the deeper, neurodivergent-informed research, I was absolutely *shook up*. I had no idea. Executive dysfunction. Emotional dysregulation. Rejection Sensitive Dysphoria. Time blindness. Sensory overwhelm. Neurodivergent meltdowns and shutdowns. ADHD Paralysis. Bottom-up processing. A deeply ingrained sense of justice.

And even T-Rex arms? (which we both have)

I was blown away. And that's putting it mildly.

As I read the symptoms, I felt like I was reading *our* story. Not in a vague, maybe-this-applies way—but in a visceral, "Oh my God, how is this all so accurate?" way. I had thought we were dealing with trauma, behavioral issues, and emotional intensity. But I was beginning to realize we were navigating an entire neurological framework I didn't even know existed.

Everything shifted.

After you pay the money and complete the Amen Clinic's incredibly thorough process, you receive an incredibly comprehensive treatment plan. It includes everything—supplements, dietary support, therapeutic recommendations, lifestyle changes, strategies for home and school. It's a full manual for care.

But the doctor was honest: none of it would matter until we got Keleigh's system to settle down a few notches. Until then, all the strategies in the world would be worthless. Her brain was in crisis mode, so he recommended we start with medication.

The recommendation wasn't based on a checklist of symptoms —it was based on what we could actually see happening in her brain. I trusted the process. But I was still a little nervous.

Keleigh, on the other hand, was totally unimpressed. She wasn't hopeful, and she didn't believe anything could help her. She was barely hanging on. But—whether to appease me or just out of sheer exhaustion—she agreed to begin treatment.

Keleigh was only taking one medication. We didn't expect much, because we'd been through so many letdowns. But in just a few short months, we started noticing small changes. When she came up against things that used to completely unravel her—something spilled, something moved, something unexpected—she'd just say, "Oh well." We'd freeze, waiting for the familiar storm, but it didn't come. It was disorienting, and we didn't know how to respond. But the small things kept growing.

Eventually, every day, things that previously would have destroyed her passed by with calmness, insight, and sometimes even humor! Linda and I started having little check-ins, quietly swapping stories: "Did you see what she did today? Can you believe it?" We'd look at each other in stunned silence, half-joking, half-serious: "Who is this person, and where the *hell* is Keleigh?"

Keleigh felt the shift too, but she wasn't ready to say it out loud. She had spent her entire life struggling, so to have that weight lift, even a little, didn't make sense to her nervous system. She didn't know how to trust the change. But then one day, a friend of hers quietly pulled us aside and said, "She told me she's starting to feel better."

I guess I already knew she had to be feeling it—something that big can't go unnoticed—but when her friend confirmed it, a wave of relief washed over me.

I had spent so many years convinced that Keleigh wouldn't survive. I couldn't see a way through. I tried to prepare myself for the worst, bracing for the day I'd lose her. But more than anything, I was haunted by the thought that if she did die, I just didn't want her to die without knowing peace.

When I realized she was finally feeling something different—something that resembled peace—I felt like, if nothing else, we had made it far enough to give her that.

And that meant so much to me.

One medicine. (Okay—one medicine and one obsessed parent frantically learning everything about neurodivergence.) That was it. One single medication changed her life.

We were in disbelief. By that point, I'd worked as a nurse for 15 years. Linda's spent decades in behavioral health. Neither of us had ever seen anything like it. Not without the usual cycle of failed attempts, brutal side effects, and constant meds adjustments. This wasn't the slow, painful climb we'd come to expect with psychiatric meds. It wasn't just a better-than-expected outcome—it felt like a complete breakthrough. Every single day for at least a year, we found ourselves repeating a single phrase over and over to each other: *I can't believe this.*

We'd never seen her like this because until now, it hadn't been possible. It felt like we were witnessing a miracle in real time. And it wasn't just the medicine—we had a new understanding. New language and a mnew framework. We were finally learning to speak the dialect of her nervous system. We were no longer patching holes in a collapsing straw house. We had tools. We had strategies. We had *words*. We weren't fixing Keleigh. We were finally learning how to meet her where she was—and that changed everything.

However, in learning how to care for Keleigh's ADHD, I began to slowly and painfully realize that I had been living with the same symptoms my entire life. I was devastated. How had I missed this? How had everyone else missed this? I'd spent years in therapy. I'd sought help. I'd described the symptoms, but no one had ever said that it was ADHD. It wasn't subtle. My entire personality practically screams it. You can't talk to me for more than a few minutes without noticing the signs. The realization hit me like a freight train.

And then it hit me even harder. As I began to understand the genetic components of ADHD, I was devastated. My biological family is... well, a disaster. That's a whole other book. I used to think we were just dysfunctional. Chaotic. Maybe even broken. But now, I saw it differently: we were *all* wired differently. But this new understanding made me look at everything in a new way. What I had always seen as dysfunction or chaos, I started to recognize as neurodivergence. I hadn't just been struggling alone—I'd been raised by and surrounded by other neurodivergent people. No wonder my house was built from straw, it's all we had.

While Keleigh was doing much better, her struggles hadn't vanished. She still has ADHD. She still had big emotions, intense needs, and days that throw her off. But now it was manageable. The constant, suffocating intensity had gone. We could live. We could breathe. We had space to figure things out instead of being in constant reaction mode. That changed everything.

Then something strange happened: I watched Keleigh begin to live a life I didn't know was possible. I mean that literally—I didn't know it was possible to live without constant struggle, daily meltdowns, sensory overload, and unbearable overwhelm. I had never seen that in my family. I hadn't seen it in myself. So when everything started to lift for her, it was like the storm that had defined our lives finally broke, the sky opening in a way I'd never seen before. It shook me, because if it was possible for her, was it possible for me too?

Chapter 6: My Second Burnout

I thought the worst was behind us. But it turns out, when you've built your life in a straw house, the walls just keep getting blown down.

La Niña is a climate pattern that describes the cooling of sea surface temperatures in the central and eastern Pacific Ocean. La Niña shifts global weather patterns, often causing increased storms, colder winters, prolonged drought, and overall atmospheric instability. Unlike hurricanes or tornadoes, La Niña is slow-moving and long-lasting—it can persist for years, subtly reshaping entire ecosystems without dramatic fanfare. Work is my La Niña—my straw house is trying to sustain itself in a slow-moving, relentless weather pattern that is impossible to escape.

So far in this book, I've revisited the agony of personal relationships, the suffering of self-doubt, and the confusion of living without answers. But none of that comes close to the pain I've experienced trying to hold a job.

I'm a nurse with a master's degree in healthcare administration. I've worked good jobs, with good people. I've made real contributions to healthcare and my community. I've done things I'm proud of. And yet, I have cried every single day in every single job.

I don't mean I cried occasionally, or during hard seasons. I mean *every day*. I have cried at work, on my way to work, and because of work. A full decade of daily emotional torture.

There were times when I cried through the entire eight-hour shift. I would sit at my desk and quietly sob. The work wasn't bad. In fact, I mostly liked it. From an employer's perspective, I was doing well. My performance reviews were great. But I felt far from it.

In that same ten-year span, I estimate I had around 40 jobs. Yes, *forty*. Some only lasted a few days. I wouldn't even make it out of orientation before I knew I couldn't survive it. Others I pushed through for a few weeks or months. A few I held onto for a year or two out of sheer willpower, and I couldn't understand why I couldn't do them like everyone else.

That's what haunted me: *Why couldn't I just do it?* Why couldn't I clock in, do the work, and clock out like everyone else?

I couldn't explain it then, and I still have trouble now. It wasn't one specific task or a single bad boss. It wasn't burnout in the typical sense. It was something deeper. A visceral, full-body, soul-crushing torment that made me feel like I was dying.

And yet—I kept trying.

Every single day, even when I wasn't actively applying for jobs, I was searching. I'd scroll through every job site, plugging in every combination of search terms I could think of, hoping to find something—*anything*—that I could survive. Not thrive in. Not love. Just *survive*.

I used to say I hated working, because "hate" was the only word I had to describe the feeling. I actually liked some of the jobs. I was professional, and a good worker. I ran teams, managed grants, started entire programs from scratch, wrote policies like a machine—and looked damn cute while doing it. From the outside, I was a high-functioning powerhouse.

But no matter how competent I appeared, I couldn't do the jobs without breaking. My body, my brain—something in me simply couldn't sustain it. I was crying in the bathroom between meetings, dissociating at my desk, spiraling every evening, trying to recover enough to do it all again the next day. It didn't matter how skilled I was. I couldn't survive it.

That's the cost of masking. That's the cost of unsupported neurodivergence. We're praised for our resilience, our intelligence, and our innovation—but we're silently falling apart behind the scenes. Nobody sees the exhaustion it takes to *seem* okay. Nobody sees the cost of holding it all together. This is what undiagnosed, unsupported neurodivergence can look like: competent, successful, even brilliant—and completely unwell.

To this day, almost everyone I know only knows the successful, competent version of me. They see the accomplishments, the energy, the confidence. Almost no one—not friends, not coworkers, not extended family—has any idea that at home, I was collapsing. That I was nonfunctional. I was crying constantly, unable to make simple decisions, or care for myself and my child. Only Linda and Keleigh have seen that version of me. It wasn't an intentional act of deception – I had no idea I was masking; it's just a part of me. Most people wouldn't have believed me if I'd told them, and still wouldn't.

In the early years, I thought the key was to find a job I was passionate about. Something meaningful. I thought that if I loved the work enough, the pain would go away. But eventually, even that dream faded. Passion wasn't the problem. I didn't need to love a job—I just needed to *survive* it. I never did. Through it all, I kept telling myself what everyone else always said: *"Nobody likes working. Everybody hates their job."* So, I buried my distress and kept going, convinced I was weak, lazy, or broken in some way. If everyone else could do it, why couldn't I?

You know that feeling right before a severe weather event? The sky turns an ominous gray, sometimes even an eerie, yellowish hue. The clouds hang heavy and low. The wind shifts. The air becomes thick. Then, you hear it, the wind chimes start going crazy, clanging, and shrieking like they know what's coming. Objects in your yard begin to lift and scatter. You can feel it in your bones: something big is about to hit. That's what this part of the story is for me. The biggest storm of my life is about to blow through, and my straw house is no match for it.

The medicine that worked for Keleigh didn't work for me.

I searched high and low. I saw specialists. I returned to the Amen Clinic. I tried naturopaths, PCPs, psychiatrists, integrative psychiatrists, spiritual healers, somatic work, even the gynecologist! I gave everything a shot—traditional, holistic, experimental. I tried a dozen medications, maybe more, but they all failed. Many of them wrecked my quality of life. I poured time, energy, and money into every recommended supplement. A few helped in moments of high anxiety, but the magic combination that worked for Keleigh never came for me.

And then—during one intake appointment with a psychiatrist—I was listing my endless symptoms and all the things I'd tried. Halfway through, he paused and said, "You've seen all these providers and done all these things. Has anyone ever told you you're on the Autism spectrum?" No, no one had ever said that to me, and I didn't believe him. I thought this was just another quack appointment to add to the long list. I'd come in hoping for answers, and instead I got what felt like a wild, irrelevant suggestion. Autism? That didn't fit.

After the appointment, I called Linda from the parking lot. I saved the Autism part for last—almost like I didn't want to say it out loud too soon. She was shocked, too. We were both trying to make sense of it.

Before I even pulled out of the parking spot, I Googled "adult women autism symptoms," and yeah... some things felt familiar, but I wasn't what I'd call convinced. Not yet. It just didn't seem possible that something so significant could've been missed for over 40 years.

In the following months, I began to casually read up on the subject. I still didn't fully believe it, until I found the late-diagnosed community online—people sharing their lives, their thoughts, and their lived experiences. It started to sink in. A lot of their experiences sounded familiar, and the grief came crashing down. It wasn't subtle or slow —it was the kind of grief that wraps itself around your entire history and says: *"This was never your fault."*

Suddenly, I was remembering all the things people have said to me—words etched into my sense of self. I thought about the exes who screamed at me, called me crazy, accused me of things I didn't even understand. I remembered being told with venom that I was ruining my daughter. That I was unstable. That I was too much for anyone to deal with.

But it wasn't just exes. It was friends. Family. Coworkers. Therapists. People who had supposedly cared about me.

I've been called mean.
Cold.
Dramatic.
Impossible.
Hysterical.
Highly-strung.
Manipulative.
Emotionally immature.
The meanest person they'd ever met.

I've been told I was confusing. Too intense. Too sensitive.
That I was always overreacting.

That I was hard to be around. Stupid. That I drained people. Selfish. Crazy.

Too emotional.
Too passionate.
Too opinionated.
Too loud.
Too quiet.
Too needy.
Too guarded.
Too much.

And—somehow—not enough.

And for years, I believed them.

I had been labeled everything you can imagine…
Everything, it seemed, *except* autistic.

I believed that something was deeply wrong with me. I believed I *was* crazy, broken, and unlovable. I tried to fix *me*. I thought if I just worked harder—became calmer, softer, more spiritual, more grounded—I could stop people from seeing me that way. I thought I could earn acceptance by becoming more digestible.

But no matter how hard I worked, the labels stuck because no one—including me—had the right lens.

But then I did.

At first, the knowledge was a little freeing, but utterly devastating.

It meant that I had spent my entire life internalizing an incredibly negative narrative that never belonged to me. What the hell was all that healing for? I had devoted myself to yoga, journaling, hiking, therapy, shadow work, clean eating, plant medicine. You name it, I'd tried it. Not casually. Not inconsistently. I gave it everything. I followed protocols, built routines (painfully and sometimes poorly, but I did it), and created vision boards. I planned my healing with almost religious intensity, convinced that if I could just work hard enough, I would finally be okay. And now, after all that effort and striving, I was being asked to stop trying to fix myself. To accept that I was differently wired. That all these struggles might not be possible to erase.

And then, things got worse, much like a storm that won't move on. A gray, dragging, drenching storm that dumps rain until the ground gives out beneath you. At first, it was just emotional. I began to feel the weight of everything our family had been through. Not just me. Not just Keleigh. But our whole family. We're a family of girls, which makes it less surprising that we all flew under the radar. Our masking was excellent and our suffering immense.

The more I learned about neurodivergence, the more I realized it was woven into every corner of my upbringing—the chaos, the emotional intensity, the confusion, the isolation. Suddenly, everything made sense. And with that understanding came another wave of grief.

Grief for everything we lived through. Grief for how deeply we were misunderstood. Grief for all the time we spent trying to be someone else.

I wanted answers, so I was still seeing every doctor, therapist, or specialist I could find. I needed something—anything—to make sense. But all I ever heard was some version of: "There's nothing wrong with you." "You're doing everything right." "I don't have any suggestions."

It wasn't that I was resistant to care—I was doing all the things. I was the poster child for lifestyle medicine, and I was getting worse. This wasn't just fatigue. It was something deeper, heavier, and harder to describe. I couldn't think clearly. I couldn't form complete sentences. I was more than tired—I couldn't function.

Prior to this, I had been running an entire healthcare facility. I worked full-time, sometimes more, while raising multiple children. How did I go from that to not being able to fold a load of laundry or answer a simple question?

I could no longer care for myself or Keleigh. Linda had to take care of both of us. There were days I couldn't get out of bed.

Days I couldn't speak. Sometimes, I was catatonic—like my body shut down and I was trapped inside it.

I could use the restroom independently and still managed to feed myself if Linda brought me food. But that was it. I spent every day crying. My executive functioning was gone. My emotional regulation—gone. My ability to cook, plan meals, or make even the smallest decisions—gone. When Keleigh would ask me something, all I could say was, *"I'm sorry, honey. I can't figure that out right now. We'll have to ask Linda."* I couldn't figure out how to respond to the simplest and most routine of questions.

I was sleeping twelve to fourteen hours a day. If I wasn't sleeping, I was crying. If I wasn't crying, I was frozen.

Eventually, I went to the ER (which as a nurse, is something we *never* do). I was convinced something had to be wrong. This couldn't just be stress or burnout. Maybe it was my thyroid. Maybe a vitamin deficiency. A tumor. Something had to be happening.

But after a full workup, the answer came back: nothing is seriously wrong with you. Probably a virus, making you feel tired. It was laughable, but at least I had more information to understand what was happening.

At some point during this period, I ordered a small $12 workbook on autistic burnout. When it arrived, I didn't rush to open it. It sat around in the box for a while, just another thing I didn't have the energy for. But one day, I idly flipped it open and was stunned. Shocked doesn't even fully capture it. I was already convinced I was impacted by neurodivergence, but this was like reading my autobiography. Every sentence described me with precision. It was the first time I saw my experience spelled out so clearly, and I couldn't deny it.

From them on, I understood not just intellectually, but viscerally. I wasn't just tired. I wasn't just overwhelmed. I was in neurodivergent burnout, and this was exactly what it looked like.

Around this time, I started to feel a sense of déjà vu, like I'd been trapped in this nightmare before. And then it hit me like a lightning bolt: I *had* been here before. It was the same desperate place we barely survived when Keleigh was a baby. And suddenly, everything made sense. I was in neurodivergent burnout then too. For the first time, I could finally release some of the horrendous shame I've carried about how our life was back then. We weren't failing. Our house was collapsing, and I hadn't even known we were in a damn storm.

What happens next unfolds slowly—but for the sake of this story, I'll sum it up like this: I had to change my whole damn life.

I had to quit working. I had to figure out how in the world I was going to survive without a job. I filed for bankruptcy. I had to reimagine *everything*—my day-to-day life, my expectations, my identity. I had to learn how to accommodate myself, which wasn't easy at all.

Once Linda fully grasped the gravity of what I was going through, she quickly adapted. She understood what I needed before I did, and still does. And honestly? I probably never would've made those changes if I hadn't completely collapsed.

Chapter 7: The Rebuild — This Time I Use a Blueprint and Bricks

The house was gone—razed to the ground. There was nothing left to patch up or salvage. In the silence that followed, the first brick I found was a single word that changed everything.

It's hard to describe the shock when I understood the meaning of *alexithymia*. It wasn't a mild "oh, that's interesting" kind of moment. It was like lightning cracking through my entire history, lighting up every corner I had spent years stumbling around in the dark.

Difficulty identifying and describing one's own emotions.

There it was.

It explained what no therapist, guide, or spiritual teacher could, what no amount of journaling had ever managed to fix. It explained why Linda always said she couldn't feel me, no matter how hard I tried to get closer. It explained why I could describe a situation in perfect detail but couldn't tell you how it made me feel. It explained why I had spent *eighteen straight months* journaling about emotions—using an emotion wheel every single day—and the only emotion that ever led me to was being ticked off that I couldn't find any emotion that I was looking for!

And I had felt *angry* about it. Dejected. Deeply frustrated. Because I was doing all the right things. Everything I had been told would help me connect with my emotions I had tried. Not casually, but diligently. I worked at it like my life depended on it, but nothing changed. The emotion wheel would stare back at me like a test I hadn't studied for. I couldn't get to what everyone else just knew.

I wasn't hiding my emotions.
I wasn't repressed.
I wasn't broken.

I was autistic—and I had *alexithymia*. Suddenly, it all made sense.

The relief was immediate and massive. For years, I felt like I'd been straining to force open a locked door, believing something essential waited behind it, only to discover it hadn't even been locked.

This wasn't something I could fix. It wasn't something I needed to *heal*. It was just how I was wired. And for the first time in my life, I could stop trying to solve it.

Now Linda had clarity, too. For so long, we believed there was something *missing,* and we blamed me for not finding it. But it turns out it wasn't personal—it was neurological.

The freedom of that realization is still unfolding.

But my new understanding didn't give me energy. I was deep in autistic burnout, and it wasn't easing up. If anything, it felt worse than before. More stubborn. More cellular. My system had fully shut down, and no amount of awareness could speed up the healing.

Recovery, I was learning, isn't about bouncing back. It's about moving forward on entirely new terms; if you return to the same life that broke you, it'll just break you again. This time, we knew there was no going back.

The only way to recover was through rest. Real rest. The kind that doesn't just mean chocolate bars, naps, and baths (though there were plenty of those), but also a radical, soul-level reduction in demands. The stripping away of everything that had asked me to pretend. I couldn't go back to "functioning" in the way I once had, because that version of me had collapsed and wasn't coming back.

Linda understood the assignment before I did. She didn't just help me survive this burnout—she became the architect of my rebuilding. While I was still frozen and trying to make sense of it all, *she* was doing the work of adjusting the structure of our life. Lowering expectations. Removing tasks. Filtering the world so it came in slower and softer. She made space for me to rest without guilt, to be nonfunctional without shame, to heal without needing to prove I was healing.

She was better at accommodating me than I was at accommodating myself, and still is to this day. I've certainly got better, but I still carry that internal pressure, that compulsion to do more, be better, get back to some version of "normal." But Linda doesn't let me go back. She reminds me, gently and persistently, that the goal is not to return. It is to rebuild something new and sustainable. Something that will hold me, not break me.

Slowly (because I can be a tad stubborn), I began to believe her.

Brick by brick, I began to feel better. At first, the changes were small—there was just a little less crying, then a few days without crying, and it kept going until eventually, I reached a place I had never known before: I didn't cry at all (unless appropriate). Not because I was numb or suppressing anything, but because I simply didn't have the feeling of constant emotional collapse. And then I started to laugh again.

That part genuinely surprised me. I didn't just stop crying—I started laughing more. Genuinely. Often. And the realization that I was spending more time laughing than crying—I didn't even know was *possible*.

Then there was another shift: I started to look forward to the future. I wasn't just tolerating or barely surviving life; I was actually *looking forward to the future*! I had never known that feeling before. I had heard of it, but I hadn't actually felt it. I hadn't given it too much thought, but I'm not even sure if I thought it was real prior to this. But here it was, growing slowly but steadily.

Way less crying.
Way more laughing.
Hope for the future.

That's not just healing—that's a *whole new life*. But it wasn't just me that needed that level of accommodation.

Keleigh's life needed even more. The changes we were making for me turned out to be exactly what she needed, too: a slower pace, a calmer environment, fewer expectations. More space to be exactly who she is, without the pressure to mask or conform. And while she does really well overall, she still has some struggles. She's still living in a world that wasn't built for her brain. Even with all the progress, insight, and support, we still see how much effort it takes for her to exist in a neurotypical world.

Linda is not only my biggest supporter, she's Keleigh's, too. She shows up for her in ways she's never had to show up for our other children. She's studied, observed, listened, and adjusted. She's the absolute best mom, the kind of parent every child deserves; patient, tuned in, unwavering. She meets Keleigh where she is, again and again, and helps her navigate life with a kind of calm certainty that's unparalleled.

Eventually, I noticed something else—something subtle, but huge.

Keleigh and I were no longer constantly triggering each other's overwhelm. We weren't stuck in that endless loop of escalation and dysregulation. Not all the time, anyway. Now, we spend real time together—*good* time. We listen to music, ride around town, and laugh. We laugh a lot. That's something we had never really been able to enjoy.

Sometimes—not always, but sometimes—we're even able to co-regulate each other instead of co-dysregulate. We can feel when the other is slipping, and instead of spiraling, we ground. We breathe. We hold space. We *show up*.

That shift alone will change the trajectory of both of our lives.

She is finally getting the kind of childhood so many of us can only dream of. A life with understanding and joy. With room to be exactly who she is, and loved for it. And I'm getting to be the kind of parent I always wanted to be. Not perfect. But *present* and connected.

Now I'd like to share a memory with you that took place in our car, the same place Keleigh first told me she wanted to die. Only this time, we weren't driving in crisis. We were just talking. She was sharing thoughts about her future—college, career paths, ideas she might want to explore. It was the first time she had ever really talked like that. The first time she let herself imagine a future.

We tossed around a few ideas. I asked her a question—I don't even remember exactly what I said—and she answered with a kind of matter-of-fact softness that nearly stopped my heart.

"You know, Mom, I never thought I'd live this long… so I don't exactly know yet."

I looked at her and replied, *"Honestly, I didn't either. But I'm so damn glad you have. Let's just keep thinking about it."*

It was the opposite of all those desperate moments. The ones when I was terrified she wouldn't survive and I didn't know how to keep her safe. This was a glimmer instead of a trigger; a full-circle moment. For the first time, we weren't bracing for what might go wrong. We were wondering what could go right.

Which makes me wonder.

Can you imagine if I had known about alexithymia before? That my struggle to name my feelings wasn't emotional damage or spiritual blockage—it was just how my brain processes emotions. A world where I understood executive dysfunction and didn't call myself lazy. Where I knew that shutdown wasn't failure, that meltdowns weren't immaturity, and that sensory overwhelm wasn't something to be ashamed of. A world where I didn't spend years believing I was too much and not enough in the same breath.

What if I'd understood bottom-up processing? What if I'd known that I wasn't bad at big-picture thinking—I just had to start with the details first? Can you imagine if I'd known about PDA? That the way my child was struggling wasn't defiance but a wired-in threat response. That the panic she felt wasn't a personality flaw but a survival instinct. That she didn't need to be fixed, she needed to be understood.

Can you imagine how different life would have been if I'd known about the oven knobs? Or that my traits weren't set to "always" or "never," but could shift depending on stress, context, and support. That some days the volume would be low, and I could pass for typical, and on other days, every dial would be cranked to high, and I'd barely make it out of bed. That everything was dynamic and part of the picture, not proof of failure.

Can you imagine if I had known about my absence of intuitive social processing?

That the reason I kept ending up in painful or abusive relationships wasn't because I was naïve or reckless—it was because my brain doesn't flag danger in a neurotypical way.

If I'd known those things, I wonder how much less pain I would have experienced.

All those years I spent trying to trust my gut, not knowing my gut didn't always speak the same language as everyone else's? How much trauma could have been prevented, if I had known, early on, that I needed help to see the signs?

I wonder how different things would have been if I had known how to accommodate myself, not just in crisis, but from the start. If I had been taught to build a life that worked with my brain, instead of always pushing against it? I wonder how differently I could have shown up in the world if I hadn't spent decades fighting to survive.

That's exactly what I'm building now for me, my daughter, and for every generation that comes after us. No more straw houses. We will live in—and pass on—brick houses with sturdy foundations.

Author's Note

Neurodivergence is real.

It's not a fad or an excuse. It's not an over diagnosis, trendy, or something that just happens because of social media. And no, it's not that "everyone is a little autistic." People say that, often with kindness or curiosity—but it entirely misses the point.

This isn't about quirks. It's about how we experience the world. It's about the real challenges we face, the exhaustion of masking, the years of misdiagnosis, the deep shame we've carried for struggling in systems that were never built for us.

None of the neurotypical methods, or advice I was given, helped. In many cases, it hurt. The only time things started to change was when I began looking through a neurodivergent lens—when I stopped trying to fix myself and developed understanding.

That's how I know this isn't a fatal flaw. It's neurodivergence. And that distinction has saved my life.

If you've read this far, you know the cost of being misunderstood and the beauty of finally being seen. You know how much is possible when we stop trying to fit and start learning how to thrive.

Our stories are real.
Our needs are real.
Our lives are real.

"We build with what we have —
straw, sticks, or brick —
and sometimes the house falls
before we ever learn
we were architects at all."

— Lish Greiner

Part Two — Blueprint for Weathering the Storms of Neurodivergent Life

Overview

Alexithymia

Auditory Processing Disorder

Bottom-up Thinking

Communication Styles and Language Differences

Difficulty (or Inability to) Change, Transition or Switch Gears

Eating and Food

Echolalia

Emotional Dysregulation

Executive Dysfunction

Invisible Disability Paradox

Interest Based Systems

Interoception Challenges

Lack of Intuitive Social Processing

Late Diagnosis/Misdiagnosis

Masking/Camouflaging

Monotropism/Hyperfocus

Neurodivergent System Overload

    Neurodivergent Overwhelm

    Neurodivergent Meltdown

    Neurodivergent Shutdown

    Neurodivergent Burnout

Object and People Impermanence

Persistent Drive for Autonomy/Pathological Demand Avoidance (PDA)

Proprioception Challenges

Rejection Sensitive Dysphoria (RSD)

Routine

Sensory Processing Differences (SPD)

Sleep Irregularities

Social-Relational Layers

Special Interest

Spiky Skills

Stimming

Strong Sense of Justice

Swiss Cheese Memory

The Paradox of Being Neurodivergent

The Weight of Being Misunderstood

Time Blindness

Introduction

By now, you know that the house I built kept collapsing. You've walked with me through the rubble, through the diagnoses that never came, through the unbearable days of not knowing what was wrong or how to help my daughter or myself. While I don't have a PhD or a long list of letters after my name, I do have the credentials that matter most for what comes next: lived experience.

Every insight in this next section was paid for in full by overstimulated mornings, shutdown afternoons, masked smiles, many jobs, burnt-out nights, and years of trial and error. This is the blueprint I wish I'd had all along.

It's a breakdown of common neurodivergent traits, experiences, concepts, and language — organized alphabetically — showing how they present in real life, what helps, what doesn't, and what radical acceptance has given. Some entries are quick definitions that deserve to be named. Others are deep dives into the layered, often invisible realities of living in a neurodivergent body and mind, in my experience. You might not share every trait or experience, but you are likely to find some reflection of yourself — or someone you love. Maybe, just maybe, it will help you to build your own sturdier house.

Not every accommodation works the same for every brain. What's life-changing for one person might be useless or even stressful for another. Some strategies work beautifully one day and fall flat the next. That's the nature of neurodivergence: inconsistent capacities, often tied to shifting internal resources, and layered with endless nuance. So, take what works, skip what doesn't, and stay open to trying things your way. You may even read something here that sparks a new idea I haven't mentioned—and that's the whole point. The blueprint is yours to build.

This blueprint isn't just about tips and tricks (though you'll find plenty). It's about language. About naming the unnamed. About learning to speak of ourselves and our loved ones with accuracy, compassion, and pride.

The right vocabulary is powerful. When we can name our experiences, we begin to understand them. When we understand them, we stop fighting ourselves. We stop blaming our children. We stop trying to fix what was never broken and instead start building what we need.

What follows is a new kind of structure. Not one patched together with shame and survival, but one rooted in understanding, acceptance, and real support. A structure where accommodations are not crutches, but tools. Where difference is not a diagnosis, but a truth, a strength, and a reality to be honored.

This is how we rebuild.

Brick by brick.
Word by word.
Trait by trait.

Alexithymia

Definition: difficulty in experiencing, expressing, and describing emotional responses.

What it feels like:

Alexithymia is something I experience deeply and consistently. Like most neurodivergent traits, it can show up differently for everyone. For me, there are certain emotions—thankfully not many—that I've never felt. I have no internal reference point for them; they just don't register. Most other emotions I feel only faintly; they skim the surface but rarely sink in.

Discovering alexithymia was a pivotal revelation on my journey. I never would have uncovered it on my own—my wife was the one who kept gently (and sometimes not-so-gently) pointing it out, again and again, until I finally began to unravel the experience.

I now understand that I don't *feel* emotions, the way most people do—I *think* feelings. Instead of sensing an emotion and reacting from that emotional place, I process things cognitively. I pause and wonder, *how should I be feeling right now? What would most people feel in this situation?* And then I respond accordingly. I didn't realize I was doing this—and I definitely didn't realize that everyone else *wasn't* doing this.

Other times, though, I don't even go through that mental checklist. There's just… nothing. No feeling. No question about what I should be feeling. I may not even realize that a feeling is expected at all. To others, this often looks like coldness, disinterest, or emotional detachment—and people usually don't respond well to that. It creates a mismatch between what I *internally* experience (or don't) and what people expect me to outwardly express, especially in moments that seem like they should carry emotional weight. Sometimes, it even happens in situations where I genuinely care. The care is real—I just don't always feel it in a way I can access or express.

To further the complication, being socialized as a girl taught me to prioritize emotional harmony, keep others comfortable, and perform the "right" feelings—whether I felt them or not. When someone suggested how I might be feeling, especially in therapy, I didn't just consider it. I adopted it and clung to it. Not because it fit, but because I had no better answer and it was the expectation.

To make things even more confusing, being neurodivergent also means I experience *extreme emotional dysregulation.* While I often feel emotionally flat or disconnected, emotions also often hit with overwhelming intensity. It's not one or the other, it's both. I can go from feeling nothing at all to being completely hijacked by a feeling I can't name, explain, or regulate. It's a messy mix of cognitive over-processing, emotional blanks, and emotional floods. Trying to make sense of it all can feel impossible.

Looking back, I see how often I confused survival-based emotional performance with true self-awareness. It's subtle and slippery. It took years to begin teasing it apart. But naming it has been one of the most validating and transformative steps in my self-understanding.

What didn't help:

Almost everything. At least not in the beginning. Not before I had the right framework, language, or self-understanding. I spent years working hard in therapy trying to "connect to my emotions." I journaled daily. I meditated. I did inner child work. I stared at emotion wheels and asked myself the "right" questions. But nothing ever really changed, because I wasn't emotionally shut down or suppressing difficult feelings—I was experiencing alexithymia, and no one around me knew how to recognize it.

Most therapists didn't just miss it; they made it worse. Many blamed my past, my mother, or even my wife. They pathologized my emotional disconnection as avoidance, resistance, or trauma repression. I had one psychologist laugh in my face—literally laugh—when I couldn't articulate how I felt about something she asked. That same therapist once asked me how I got over the anger from an ex-girlfriend who had beaten me nearly to death on more than one occasion. I responded, a little confused, "Oh… I was never mad at her." She looked at me and said, "Well, that's weird." I saw that therapist for an extended period of time, and this topic came up during nearly every single session. Not once did she ever mention alexithymia.

That kind of harm lingers. It made me doubt myself more than I did already. It made me feel broken in ways I wasn't. It kept me stuck in the exhausting loop of trying to feel things the way I thought I was supposed to, without understanding that my brain just doesn't work that way.

What does help:

Understanding how my brain is wired.

Learning about alexithymia was one of the most validating discoveries of my neurodivergent journey. It explained so much—not just about how I experience emotions, but why so many things in my past didn't make sense. Why therapy felt so frustrating, and why I often felt like I was somehow doing life wrong. This understanding brought a kind of peace I didn't know was possible.

Even now, I sometimes wonder if I'm missing something that everyone else seems to feel. But when that happens, I remind myself: I'm not missing anything. I'm just living it differently. That's okay. That's how I'm built.

It's also been transformative in my relationship with Linda. When we both came to understand alexithymia, she no longer felt like I wasn't connecting with her—she just came to see that I connect in a different way than she expected. Previously, she was looking for the emotional cues and signals two neurotypical people might share. Because I wasn't offering those, it *felt* like absence. But it wasn't. That shift in understanding brought so much relief for both of us.

What's been most freeing is letting go of the constant, exhausting pressure to find emotions that don't exist, or to contort myself into someone I'm not just to prove that I care, or feel.

Try the tools that are out there—emotion wheels, body scans, journaling prompts. Sometimes they may help. But if they don't seem to land—if you're still searching, or if you feel like you've hit a wall or reached a plateau—let acceptance in. You may not be broken. You may just be *different*. And that difference is worthy of care, respect, and peace.

Accommodations:

Alternative Ways to Show Emotional Connection

If you're someone who struggles to *feel* or *express* emotions in the typical way, that doesn't mean you're incapable of love, empathy, or deep connection. It just means you may need different tools to communicate those things—and the people close to you may need help learning to recognize them.

Here are some ways I've learned to show emotional connection:

- Acts of service. Doing something helpful, thoughtful, or caring—like making coffee, fixing something, making someone's favorite meal, or anticipating a need—can be a powerful way to say "I care" without using emotional language.
- Sharing space. Just being near someone, choosing to spend time together, or inviting them into your routines can be your way of expressing love and connection.
- Checking in intellectually. I may not always *feel* what someone else is feeling, but I ask questions, stay curious, and offer ideas or solutions. That's often how I express care.
- Creating systems. I show love through structure—scheduling things that support someone I love, remembering their preferences, or organizing things in a way that makes life smoother for them.
- Rituals and habits. Predictable touchpoints—like a nightly check-in, a morning text, or watching a favorite show together—can hold as much emotional weight as any deep conversation.

- Name what's true. Sometimes I simply say: "I may not express it the way you expect, but I love you, and I'm here." That sentence has bridged more gaps than I ever expected.

Connection doesn't have to look like big emotions, tears, or poetic declarations. It can be quiet, steady, practical, or even awkward. What matters is that it's real.

Radical acceptance:

For me, radical acceptance meant finally understanding that I wasn't broken, I was just different. It meant releasing the idea that if I tried hard enough, I could learn to feel like everyone else. It meant grieving the emotional fluency I thought I *should* have, and the ways I used to beat myself up for not being "connected enough."

Radical acceptance doesn't mean giving up—it means giving in to the truth of your wiring. It means saying, "Okay, this is how I work," and letting that be enough.

It's the difference between *chasing* emotions you can't access and trusting the ways you already show up—with presence, curiosity, care, and commitment.

In my closest relationships, it's meant being seen and accepted without having to perform connection in a way that doesn't fit. That's where healing really lives.

Auditory Processing Differences (APD)

Definition: A neurological condition where the brain has difficulty processing sounds—including spoken language—even with normal hearing. Individuals with Auditory Processing Disorder (APD) may struggle to understand speech, especially in noisy environments, and have trouble with tasks like following directions or remembering spoken information. Because the brain has trouble filtering and prioritizing sounds, all auditory input can come in at the same level of importance or intensity—making it difficult to focus on one voice or sound while tuning out background noise. This condition often overlaps with sensory processing differences, particularly those involving auditory sensitivity and filtering.

What it feels like:

Auditory Processing Disorder makes it hard for my brain to interpret spoken language in real time. Sometimes, when someone is talking to me, it feels like they're speaking another language—my brain scrambles the input or lags behind, trying to catch up. (The neurodivergent brain is often taking in way more than the neurotypical brain—some estimates say as much as 42% more.) That's why, for example, if you say you want a banana, I might blurt out something totally unrelated, like "What did the Queen of England do thrice?" There's just a lot happening in my head, and sometimes it gets scrambled.

When this happens, people often assume I wasn't listening, or worse, that I'm being dismissive or making a joke. In reality, it's a delay. I usually *do* hear the words, but it takes a beat (or several) for them to register and unscramble. However, by the time my brain has caught up, the other person is already repeating themselves in frustration, while I'm suddenly trying to respond to what I've finally processed. It leads to a confusing back-and-forth that doesn't make sense.

Over the years, this has caused friction in my relationships. It's also caused some hilarious moments, because the things I mishear are often wildly off base and absurd. But when there's a lack of understanding, especially from people who expect "normal" conversational timing, it can lead to misunderstandings, conflict, and assumptions that I'm not paying attention or don't care.

The experience must be so hard for children with auditory processing differences and parents or teachers who don't understand. Constantly being told you're rude, disrespectful, or "not listening," when in fact your brain just needs more time to decode sound, can lead to shame and self-doubt. It can also mask deeper needs that never get addressed, because no one's looking at how the brain is functioning. (I have almost no memory of my childhood, so while I can't recall specifics, I do remember one of my parents frequently being mad at me for constantly asking "what?")

The second part of this definition has caused me a lot of struggle, pain, and overwhelm—and has often impacted my relationships. It feels like there's no volume knob or sorting system for sound—everything arrives all at once and at the same intensity. The hum of the refrigerator, a conversation across the room, a car passing by, footsteps in the hallway, and the person speaking directly to me all compete equally for attention.

For most of my life, I didn't realize this was different. When you've always lived this way, you assume everyone else is experiencing the world the same. But once I learned that other people's brains automatically filter and prioritize sounds, I began to see just how much mine was working against me. During burnout, when my resources were low and my skills regressed, that difference became impossible to ignore—the volume seemed to turn up on everything at once, pun absolutely intended.

For a neurotypical brain, that filtering happens instinctively—their system decides what matters and fades the rest into the background. For us, it doesn't. We either can't filter or we have to do it manually, and even that takes a tremendous amount of effort. Something as ordinary as having a conversation in a restaurant becomes an act of intense concentration and endurance.

This constant manual filtering is one of the many ways our internal resources are used differently. Tasks that seem effortless for others can leave us depleted—because we're processing more. And when you don't know that others aren't living this way, it's easy to blame yourself or assume you're "too sensitive." Then, when the noise finally becomes too much and your system hits overload, people see only the reaction. They call you moody, rude, or overdramatic—without realizing you've simply run out of resources to keep holding it all together.

Auditory Processing Disorder isn't a hearing problem. It's a brain processing disorder. With the right understanding, patience, and accommodations, conversations can feel so much easier for everyone.

Accommodations:

Auditory Processing Disorder isn't about hearing loss; it's about how the brain processes sound. That means the most helpful accommodations are about *how* communication happens, not *what* is being said. The goal isn't to simplify the message, it's to make sure it has space and structure to land.

And because the brain doesn't automatically filter sounds in the expected way, background noise and even subtle environmental sounds can compete at the same level as the person speaking. Accommodations that reduce auditory load aren't just helpful—they're essential for preserving energy, focus, and emotional regulation.

Here are a few accommodations that can make a big difference:

- Give time. Allow a pause after speaking. If I don't respond right away, it's not that I'm ignoring the person speaking to me— I'm still decoding their words.
- Reduce background noise. Competing sounds makes it much harder to process language. If possible, turn off the TV, move to a quieter space, or limit overlapping conversations.
- Use earplugs or noise-reducing headphones. I can't stress this one enough! I didn't even know I needed them until I got a pair for Keleigh and ordered my own on a whim. I carry them with me everywhere! They've changed my life—helping me quiet the world enough to think, focus, and stay regulated.
- Use visual or written cues. When possible, pair spoken language with gestures, text, or written instructions. Seeing the words can help solidify what was heard.

- Confirm gently. Instead of repeating something in frustration, ask, "Did that make sense?" or "Do you want me to say that another way?"
- Avoid rapid-fire instructions. Break tasks into steps and communicate them one at a time using speech, pictures, or writing.
- Signal when something important is coming. A cue like "Hey, I need your focus for this next part" can help shift attention and prepare the brain to absorb the information.
- Practice patience and humor. Sometimes what I hear is so wildly off, I just have to laugh. Making space for humor makes the misfires feel less stressful for everyone.

These aren't just tips, they're access points. When used with care, they open communication that doesn't rely on speed, but on presence and mutual respect.

Radical Acceptance:

With Auditory Processing Disorder, radical acceptance isn't about embracing deep emotional truth—it's more about releasing the guilt and confusion that can come from always being "off" in conversations. It's accepting that sometimes I'll respond too slowly or say something that makes no sense at all. But it doesn't mean I'm not trying or listening. It just means my brain is doing its own kind of processing.

Radical acceptance also means knowing that I don't need to perform neurotypical listening to be worthy of respect. I've spent a lot of time feeling bad for being "difficult to talk to," when really, I just need a different rhythm. Accepting that has made space for so much more ease and allowed me to self-advocate without shame.

It also means accepting that the world sounds different to me than it does to others. What overwhelms me might barely register for someone else—not because I'm too sensitive, but because my brain isn't filtering in the same way. Recognizing that difference has been freeing. It helps me extend compassion to myself when noise or chaos feels unbearable and reminds me that it's not a character flaw—it's a neurological difference. Finding tools that honor that difference, like my earplugs, has been life-giving; they offer me moments of calm in a world that often feels too loud for me to live in without draining all of my resources.

Bottom-Up Processing

Definition: Bottom-up processing is a way of understanding and responding to the world that starts with raw input—sensory details, physical sensations, environmental cues, and emotional signals—and builds *upward* into meaning, context, and response. Rather than starting with a big-picture understanding or assumption and filtering details through that lens (as in top-down processing), bottom-up processing gathers *all* the details first to create the big picture.

For bottom-up thinkers, the path to understanding is through observation, pattern recognition, and immersion in the moment. It can feel like assembling a puzzle without the picture on the box—you don't know what it *is* until you've examined enough pieces.

This often means:

- Needing to experience something firsthand before it "makes sense."
- Being highly tuned to context, tone, body language, and environment
- Feeling overwhelmed by too much input—or deeply grounded by subtle sensory cues
- Having insights or emotional responses arise *after* the moment has passed.

Bottom-up processing is common in neurodivergent people, and it's not less efficient, it's just a different route to understanding. The picture may take longer to assemble, but the results are often richer and more nuanced.

Top-down processing is how most neurotypical people tend to operate. It starts with prior knowledge, expectations, or mental shortcuts—essentially a big-picture framework—and uses that to interpret new information. It's fast and efficient but often filters out details that don't match the narrative. Neither system is better or worse, but they operate differently. The differences can create major communication gaps between neurodivergent and neurotypical people.

What it feels like:

At first glance, this might seem like a small detail, but it's actually *huge*. Bottom-up processing shapes how I take in the world, communicate, learn, relate to others, and how I function in just about every environment. Yet most people, especially neurotypical people, have no idea it exists.

People who aren't bottom-up thinkers often find us exhausting, interruptive, scattered, or overly literal. Maybe even "too much." While they're zooming out and filtering for meaning based on prior experience, we're zooming in, gathering as many details as we can to build understanding.

In conversation, this difference can create confusion. A bottom-up thinker might interrupt—not to be rude—but because something doesn't make sense yet and they need to clarify before they can keep listening. We're not arguing. We're *processing*. And that difference matters. Once I understood this about myself, it made such a big difference.

Top-down thinkers are fast. They rely on pattern recognition, intuition, and prior knowledge to move through life efficiently, and that can be incredibly useful. Bottom-up thinkers often see what others miss. Because we're not filtering out "irrelevant" data, we're more likely to notice contradictions, nuance, context shifts, or new possibilities.

Some of the most visionary people in history—innovators, artists, scientists, inventors—have been bottom-up thinkers. We're not wired to just accept the rules, and that often means we come up with ideas that are out of the box—because we were never in the box.

Truly understanding this difference has radically improved my communication with others. It has taken the personal sting out of so many past interactions. I wasn't being combative or difficult. I was just processing differently.

What it can look like when I'm processing bottom-up:

- Interrupting to clarify a detail that doesn't yet make sense

- Seeming overly focused on "irrelevant" information

- Asking lots of questions before I can respond

- Appearing slow to grasp something (because I'm processing every detail)

- Taking longer to form an opinion or decision

- Seeming like I "always want to be right"—but I actually just want the facts to be accurate so I can process them

- Struggling with vague statements or incomplete information

- Being quiet while my brain sorts things out

- Not understanding implied meanings or assumptions until they're made explicit

What didn't help:

Being rushed. When I feel like someone is expecting a quick answer or trying to move the conversation along faster than my brain can process, everything inside me starts to scramble. My thoughts get jumbled, my words disappear, and suddenly I can't think straight. The more pressure I feel to "hurry up," the slower and more chaotic my brain becomes. There's just so much to sort through—sensory input, emotional tone, the content of what's being said—and when I'm rushed, it all becomes noise.

Interestingly, this mostly shows up outside of work—particularly in relationships or unstructured interactions. In work settings, especially in nursing, I actually excelled. That's because there were clear rules, policies, and expectations—structures I could memorize and operate within. Once I understood a framework, there was almost nothing I couldn't figure out. In fact, I was known for moving through tasks with speed and precision. But this same bottom-up style that made me effective in my job, also made me incredibly frustrating to work with. Before making a decision, I would have to investigate every detail, read every note in a patient's chart, talk to everyone involved, and make sure I had the full picture. To me, that was how good care happened. To others, it felt like overkill—or worse, like I was trying to check up on people or catch them doing something wrong. They didn't understand that I *needed* all the pieces before I could confidently act. As a result, I caught errors and understood the nuances of patients' needs. But socially, it made me feel isolated, resented, and misunderstood.

It also doesn't help when people skip over details they think aren't important, over-generalize, or assume I already know what they mean. When people leave things vague or imply that I should already understand, I end up feeling lost or like I'm missing something obvious—because I probably am, not because I'm slow or careless, but because I need the *whole picture* before I can find meaning.

I've often been misunderstood in personal relationships. My bottom-up processing wasn't just seen as inefficient or annoying—it was interpreted as a character flaw. People assumed I was being controlling, difficult, obsessive. They saw my attention to detail as micromanaging, my need for clarity as criticism, my questions as distrust.

It's like a two-way street with mismatched maps. I'm thinking, *why aren't you giving me the full picture? Where are the details?* And they're thinking, *why are you asking so many questions? Why can't you just follow the general idea?* When

I try to share something in the detailed, step-by-step way my brain naturally operates, it's often met with impatience or frustration. Somehow, the bottom-up thinker ends up being the one seen as "wrong" for needing clarity *and* providing it. I hate saying that, but it's something I've experienced again and again. No doubt other factors are at play—personality, trauma, communication style— but this pattern has followed me everywhere. It doesn't matter how thoughtful, careful, or well-intentioned I am, people still often read it as resistance or criticism.

It's incredibly confusing to be in those conversations where you can feel the other person's frustration—sometimes quietly, sometimes loudly—and you genuinely don't understand what you did wrong. When they finally say it out loud, it's even more disorienting. You try to explain yourself, but you don't have the right words. You're still mid-process. You're not trying to be difficult, dismissive or controlling, but the other person has already decided that's what you are. And no amount of explaining seems to help. The more you try to clarify, the more misunderstood you become. What they're accusing you of doesn't match your thoughts, your intentions, or your feelings, but eventually, you realize none of that matters. What matters is how it was received, so you stop trying to explain. You accept the misinterpretation because you've learned that arguing usually just deepens the divide. The pattern of being misunderstood and having to absorb the cost of that misunderstanding just keeps happening. In friendships. In family. In work. In love. And it all chips away at your sense of being knowable.

This is why something that seems so small—a simple difference in how we process information—can quietly shape an entire life. It changes how we're read in relationships, how we're spoken to, and how we're judged. It determines whether we're seen as thoughtful or difficult, caring or cold, competent or combative. When it goes unseen or misunderstood for long enough, it can shape the story we tell ourselves.

It's not a minor trait or a communication quirk. It's a fundamental part of how we move through the world. When it's misunderstood, the impacts ripple through everything.

What does help:

The most helpful thing, hands down, has been simply knowing about bottom-up processing—and naming it. Having the words for what my brain is doing has changed everything. Before, it always felt like something was wrong with me, but once I understood that I just have a different processing style, I stopped taking it so personally—and so did the people around me. Now, when I'm in a conversation and catch someone getting frustrated because I'm asking a million questions—or I blurt out something wildly specific in the middle of someone sharing something emotional—I'll just laugh and say, "Oh sorry, I'm such a bottom-up thinker." Almost every time, people just accept it, so I don't have to give a long explanation. I don't even have to say I'm neurodivergent. The phrase itself gives them just enough of a clue, and naming it with humor and ease softens the moment. It works even better in close relationships. With Linda, it's made such a difference to know that we're not actually arguing—we're just processing differently. Instead of spiraling into hurt feelings or defensiveness, we can name what's happening in real time and adjust. It's no longer, "You're being difficult," or "You never understand me"—it's "Oh, we're coming at this from different angles." That shift has turned what used to be conflict into clarity and sometimes connection.

Accommodations:

These accommodations aren't about lowering expectations—they're about creating clarity and communication pathways that work for bottom-up thinkers.

- Give processing time. Don't rush responses. A pause after speaking gives us space to take in what was said and put together our response.
- Be specific and concrete. Vague language, metaphors, or "you know what I mean" don't always land. Clear, detailed communication helps us build understanding.
- Avoid skipping steps. Bottom-up thinkers need the full picture to make sense of something. When steps are skipped or assumptions made, we're often left confused or playing catch-up.
- Normalize clarifying questions. Repeating or rephrasing something isn't arguing—it's how we process and confirm understanding.
- Provide written communication. Writing gives us time to gather information and organize our thoughts without the pressure of real-time conversation.
- Limit multitasking in communication. Too much input at once—background noise, distractions, or too many simultaneous conversations—can overload bottom-up processors.
- Offer visual or step-by-step information. Seeing things laid out clearly can support comprehension and decision-making.
- Understand that we may need to revisit conversations. New insights often come after the moment has passed. Looping back doesn't mean rehashing—it means better understanding.

- Respect the need for detail. We're not nitpicking—we're connecting dots. Letting us access and explore those dots helps us do our best thinking. Along this same line normalize the phrase **"I'm not arguing/trying to be right, I'm just trying to understand/get all the details."** (This has been so helpful for me).
- Nurture the relationship. When people recognize and respect the differences in processing style, communication becomes less about frustration and more about collaboration. Relationships rooted in this understanding are more sustainable, compassionate, and genuinely connected.

Radical acceptance:

Radical acceptance of bottom-up processing began when I stopped trying to think like everyone else—and stopped expecting others to think like me. For a long time, I thought I was just slow, difficult, or too intense. I carried so much shame about needing more time, more information, more *everything* just to feel like I understood what was going on. I tried to push myself to keep up, stay quiet, and not "overdo it" with the details—but that only disconnected me from myself.

Accepting that my brain builds meaning from the ground up has allowed me to stop treating it as a flaw and start treating it as part of my design. It's not always easy, and the misunderstandings haven't disappeared, but they have become easier to navigate. I no longer internalize every frustrated sigh, every "you're overthinking it," and every assumption that I'm trying to argue or prove something. I'm not. I'm just processing.

I also no longer feel the need to constantly explain or justify how my brain works to people who aren't interested in understanding. Sometimes, the most compassionate thing I can do is shrug and say, "This is how I'm wired." That small act of naming it has created more peace than years of over-explaining ever did.

Communication Styles and Language Differences

For many neurodivergent people, communication doesn't follow a neurotypical script. Our language styles, timing, and word choices can be noticeably different—and often misunderstood. We're not trying to be rude, vague, overly intense, or inattentive. Our communication style is shaped by how our brains process information, feel emotions, and interpret the world.

Verbal processing is a common trait where we talk in order to think. We may not know what we believe until we say it out loud. Sometimes that looks like rambling, circling back, or even contradicting ourselves mid-sentence—not because we're indecisive, but because we're thinking in real time. Writing can work in the same way. We might not realize what we *feel* until we write it all out. The process of externalizing thoughts is how we *find* them.

Processing lag is where our brain is still working on a response while the conversation moves on without us. We may stare blankly when asked a question, go silent in conversations, or think of the perfect reply three hours later. That's not avoidance. It's just how long it takes for the thoughts and words to catch up. This delay can be especially confusing for others when the person appears to be high functioning in other ways.

Info-dumping is another frequent expression of neurodivergent communication, where we share a long stream of detailed, enthusiastic information, often about a special interest. It might come out fast, intense, or with more depth than the listener expects. We're not trying to dominate the conversation—we're offering a piece of ourselves. For many of us, this is *connection*. This is how we say, "I like you. Here's something that matters to me."

Literal thinking means that sarcasm, metaphors, idioms, and unspoken meanings don't always land the way we intend. If you say, "I'm totally dead from that workout," we might briefly wonder who died. If you say, "Don't throw the baby out with the bathwater," we might need a second to work through the image (and probably hate it). It's not that we lack imagination—it's that we often interpret things exactly as they're said, especially when tired or overwhelmed.

These differences in timing, tone, and interpretation can create friction, but they're not flaws. They're reflections of a brain that works from the bottom up, often prioritizing precision, passion, and internal logic over convention. Once understood, they can lead to incredibly rich, meaningful, and refreshingly honest communication.

Difficulty (or inability) to Change, Transition or Shift

Definition: This is the neurological challenge of shifting from one state, task, thought, emotion, or environment to another. This can include transitions between activities (like stopping play to start homework), mental states (like moving from calm to alert), physical locations (like from home to school), or even internal focus (like changing from thinking about one topic to another). For many neurodivergent people, especially those with autism or ADHD, these shifts can feel abrupt, disorienting, or even threatening—leading to resistance, shutdown, or emotional dysregulation.

At its core, this difficulty isn't about stubbornness or inflexibility. It's often a matter of cognitive load, sensory regulation, and nervous system overwhelm. Transitions require rapid adaptation—and for neurodivergent systems that thrive on predictability, deep focus, or routine, shifting gears can feel like slamming the brakes on a train. It takes time and support to stop, reset, and start again.

What it feels like:

A neurotypical brain is like a clean, well-designed highway system. The lanes are clearly marked, the signs make sense, and the exits appear exactly where you expect them to. A neurodivergent brain, on the other hand, is more like a wild, living map — a tangled network of highways, backroads, overpasses, roundabouts, and scenic detours. Some exits only appear under certain conditions. Some roads loop back on themselves, and others lead somewhere entirely unexpected. It's beautiful, but it's also chaotic — an ever-changing web of possibility and overwhelm.

So when we try to change, redirect, or transition, it's not as simple as taking the next exit. For us, change requires a full rerouting — a reorganization of the whole system. It takes longer, demands more energy, and often feels messy and sometimes isn't even possible.

That visual, for me, helps me understand why shifting from one task, role, or state to another—whether physical, emotional, or cognitive—can be very difficult. This trait is sometimes called "inertia" or "task-switching difficulty," and it's often misunderstood. People may assume we're being oppositional, lazy, or rigid, but this challenge is usually about the internal toll it takes to stop one thing, reorient, find an alternate route, and begin another. It's like hitting a sudden detour sign after miles of highway, with no clear GPS signal to guide you.

For a long time, I internalized this struggle and assumed I was rigid and controlling. But that never quite fit because my personality is actually laid back. I'm not someone who needs things to go a certain way. I don't get stuck because I'm attached to a plan—I get stuck because my brain cannot find its way in its own tangled network of roadways. It's not rigidity. It's panic. It's like being trapped in a traffic jam where every possible exit is blocked, and there's nothing I can do to arrive at my destination as planned.

When something changes unexpectedly, especially in personal or emotional situations, I often can't get from point A to point B. As a result, my system freezes.

However, in professional environments, I can often rely on the external framework—protocols, schedules, expectations—to guide me when something changes. There's structure to lean on, and that makes all the difference. It's like driving on a highway with guardrails and clear signage — I may still swerve, but I won't get lost. In the rest of life, where structure is looser and more relational, I often feel completely unmoored when a shift occurs. The adjustment doesn't just take effort—it can be impossible.

It's not just about switching activities—it's about the neurological effort involved in changing directions. Getting out of bed, leaving the house, ending a conversation, starting a new one, wrapping up a project, beginning a new task, transitioning from calm to focused, from focused to relaxed—these are all shifts. For many of us, even when the transition is expected or planned, it's still draining. Every re-route burns fuel. If there are too many transitions in a day—school drop-off, errands, appointments, cooking dinner, a conversation about bills—our limited energy is zapped. By the end of the day, we're not just tired. We're spent. Sometimes, we're so depleted that we cannot shift again, even if we want to.

It often feels like Linda comes to a fork in the road and just… turns. Maybe she expected to go left, but the moment calls for a right turn instead. She might sigh, or feel a little off for a second, but she turns. Her map updates in real time. My road doesn't even have a fork—and when it's time to shift, it's not a gentle turn, it's a full-body ordeal. I claw my way off road through a thick marsh on my hands and knees, through mud and thorns and water sometimes over my head. And even then, I may not make it to the new path. Or I might get there completely scraped up and disoriented, with nothing left in the tank to keep going.

It's not just about the change itself. It's about the internal process required to navigate it. Some people pivot, but I have to survive a whole damn expedition just to shift. It's not just changing lanes—it's building the road as I go.

This challenge is often invisible to others, and it often leads to misunderstandings. Loved ones may feel rejected when we can't pivot to meet them in a new emotional space. Teachers may think a student is being difficult when they can't move from recess to math. Partners might interpret our stuckness as avoidance, disinterest, or even passive aggression, but our systems are simply overwhelmed.

We often want to shift, we know we need to, but that doesn't mean we can. That gap between knowing and doing—that liminal stuck space—can feel maddening and filled with shame.

Radical acceptance, accommodations, and supportive scaffolding are key. For some of us, that means building in longer transition times, using gentle cues, creating rituals that help us shift states, or having trusted people talk us through the change. For others, it might mean reducing the number of daily transitions or grouping tasks together in ways that limit back-and-forth movement.

Whatever form it takes, the goal isn't to fix our difficulty with transitions—it's to support ourselves in building bridges instead of blaming ourselves for not teleporting across. We can't redesign the entire highway system in our heads, but we can put up better signs, add more rest stops, and learn where the exits actually are.

What doesn't help:

Life. Unexpected texts, last-minute plan changes, someone needing something *right now* when you were finally about to sit down—basically, existence. Neurotypical life is not designed with neurodivergent brains in mind, and the constant demands to shift, pivot, and adapt on the fly can feel like psychological whiplash. It's not resistance—it's depletion.

What also doesn't help? Rushing us. Getting frustrated. Forcing the change. All these responses might be intended to "get us moving," but they often have the opposite effect. They send our nervous systems into shutdown or spiral mode. The pressure to transition faster than our system can handle doesn't motivate—it dysregulates. And when we're dysregulated, transitions become even harder. But it's a loop we sometimes *can* navigate with gentleness, time, and support.

And here's the most insidious thing that doesn't help: the internalized belief that we *should* be able to do things differently. That we're just being dramatic. That everyone else can roll with change, so why can't we? Many of us have masked this struggle for years—forcing smiles, pushing through transitions, internalizing the meltdown. But masking doesn't make the friction go away, it just buries it, deepens our fatigue, and deepens shame. When the world tells us we're rigid or difficult, we start to believe it. But the truth is, we're not unwilling—we're overloaded. Our systems are screaming for safety, not control. Learning to hear that difference is everything.

Well-meaning suggestions rooted in neurotypical strategies for "getting over" rigidity—just reframe it, be flexible, let it go, and breathe—are also unhelpful. Those tools weren't built for brains like mine. When your nervous system is in panic mode, breathing techniques and logic rarely touch it. "Just adapt" isn't a strategy—it's a demand. When our system is already flooded, demands only push us deeper into shutdown or meltdown. The more I tried to use those tools, the more I blamed myself when they didn't work. I thought I was failing, but those tools were not designed for me.

What does help:

Gentle predictability is helpful—clear cues, prep time, soft landings, and flexible expectations. It helps to have a heads-up about what's coming next, time to process the shift, and permission to move at our own pace.

It helps when people around us stop rushing and start co-regulating. When we're met with curiosity instead of impatience. When someone says, "take your time" and means it.

Sometimes, what helps is simply naming what's hard. Saying out loud: *"I'm reaching my limit on the number of transitions I can handle for the day."* That alone can start to shift the shame because it's not weakness, it's a boundary. And boundaries are how we protect our energy, our regulation, and our relationships.

When we say it out loud, people around us have a chance to respond to what's *actually* happening, rather than reacting to the outward signs of our distress, like snippiness, avoidance, or being rigid in our thinking. Clarity helps everyone. It invites compassion instead of conflict, and that can change the whole tone.

When the tone changes, it changes how we interact with one another, and over time, it reshapes our relationships. When we're supported, we feel safer. When we feel safer, we can be more flexible, because we're regulated enough to try.

Relationships built on mutual understanding instead of constant friction are softer, stronger, and more sustainable. It's the difference between surviving each day together and enjoying those days.

Accommodations:

- Build in buffer time between tasks or activities. Avoid back-to-back plans to give space for recalibration. Transitioning takes mental and emotional energy, and we need time to shift gears.
- Use predictable transition cues or rituals. Try music, a phrase ("Okay, I'm wrapping this up"), a light change, or a specific movement to signal one thing ending and another beginning.
- Give countdowns or advance warnings. "Ten more minutes," "One more episode," "In 20 minutes I'll need your help"—phrases like these help us prepare mentally and emotionally, even as adults.
- Use visual schedules or flow charts. Seeing the day laid out can make transitions feel less jarring. Even a loose outline can provide structure.
- Preview upcoming changes. Let us know what's coming, especially if it involves a demand. "After lunch we'll go to the store," or "When you're done resting, I'll need help folding laundry."
- Incorporate anchoring actions. Repeated cues like shutting a laptop, closing a door, or writing a "pause" note help create a signal that something is ending.
- Allow processing time. If we're not moving right away, it doesn't mean we're refusing. Our brains may be busy rerouting. Silence or stillness are part of the transition.
- Use phrases to externalize capacity. Say "I'm reaching the limit on the number of transitions I can handle

today." This helps others respond with care instead of reacting to symptoms like frustration or snippiness.
- Regulate before shifting. Use sensory tools, movement, music, or stillness to regulate the nervous system. A regulated body can transition more easily.
- Limit the number of transitions when possible. Combine tasks, cancel extras, or batch errands to reduce gear-switching throughout the day.

Radical Acceptance:

I used to think I was just difficult, rigid, and resistant. Every time I froze in the face of change or shut down after a long day of switching roles and directions, I felt like I was failing. I didn't understand how other people could pivot so easily—I felt like I was clawing through quicksand just to put on shoes and get out the door.

Radical acceptance didn't make the transitions easier, but it made me be kinder to myself, and that's everything.

It starts with understanding that this isn't about stubbornness or control. It's not a personality flaw, it's a nervous system response. My brain wasn't built to smoothly switch gears, so when I expect myself to do it, I only end up feeling broken.

I stopped asking "Why can't I just be more flexible?" and started saying, "This is how my brain shifts. I don't need to feel shame."

Radical acceptance means making room for this truth, without shaming it into submission. It means preparing for transitions instead of expecting them to magically feel okay. It means forgiving myself when I hit my limit. It means building a life with fewer back-to-back expectations and more breath between the lines.

Masking this struggle for years didn't make it go away—it just made me exhausted and afraid. Afraid of being seen as dramatic. Afraid of disappointing people. Afraid of being "too much" and "not enough." Now I recognize those shutdowns and spirals as signals, not failures. My body's not betraying me, it's protecting me. It's saying: *This is too much, too fast, too soon.*

So now I listen. I build in margins. I talk to people about what I need. I forgive myself when I can't shift. I've stopped expecting myself to flip a switch that simply doesn't exist.

One of the most powerful things I've learned is this: when I speak more softly to myself—by shifting the language of my inner monologue—I speak differently out loud too. I say things with more grace, honesty, and compassion. And when I do that, people soften toward me. And often, they soften toward themselves. That's the quiet power of radical acceptance.

Eating & Food

For many neurodivergent people food isn't just about nourishment. It's deeply tied to sensory processing, executive functioning, comfort, emotional regulation, routines, dopamine, and even special interests. As a result, eating can be both a comfort and a challenge, depending on the day, the environment, or the individual's current level of regulation.

Here are some of the challenges:

- Sensory sensitivities play a major role. Certain textures, smells, tastes, or temperatures can be intolerable, while others might be deeply comforting. This can lead to extremely selective eating, sometimes misunderstood as "picky" when it's really about sensory regulation.
- Food routines may feel necessary. Eating the same meals every day can offer relief and predictability in an otherwise overwhelming world.
- Some neurodivergent people may forget to eat, eat only "safe" foods, or struggle with interoception (not recognizing hunger or fullness cues).
- Others may engage in stimming behaviors through food — crunching ice, chewing specific textures, or seeking spicy or fizzy sensations for regulation.
- Executive dysfunction can interfere with every step of eating — from planning meals, buying groceries, cooking, and remembering to eat. Often, ADHD folks go long periods without eating, only to binge later when hunger catches up.
- Dopamine-seeking plays a big role in food choices. Foods that are highly stimulating (sugar, carbs, processed foods) often feel more appealing — not because we're lazy or lack willpower, but because our brains are wired to chase stimulation to function.
- Time blindness can also make regular meals a struggle. Hours pass without awareness, and by the time hunger hits, it can feel like an emergency.
- These dynamics can collide, making food an incredibly complex terrain. You might crave novelty (ADHD) but only tolerate familiar textures (Autism). You might want to meal plan but find the thought of making that

many decisions completely overwhelming. You may cycle between total disinterest in food and hyperfixation on one specific item.

Neurodivergent people often internalize shame around their eating habits because they don't match cultural norms or expectations. Understanding the *why* behind our behaviors opens the door to compassion, accommodation, and sustainable nourishment.

The aforementioned challenges are things that I have experienced, but not in ways that particularly impacted my life greatly. I wanted to expand on two concepts around eating and food that have shown up often enough to remind me that food and regulation are deeply connected.

Sometimes I'm hungry, I know I'm hungry, but nothing seems to make sense in terms of what I could eat. I can feel the hunger clearly, yet my brain can't locate the answer—it's like the signal gets scrambled. Usually, I'll tell my wife I'm hungry, and she'll ask, *"What do you want to eat?"* I'll say, *"I don't know."* Then she'll list off seventy possibilities, and I'll respond *"no,"* *"that doesn't sound good,"* or *"I don't know"* another hundred times. It quickly becomes frustrating for both of us.

There's more happening in those moments than just hunger, executive dysfunction, overwhelm, or decision paralysis—it's also metabolic. It's hypoglycemia. I'm extremely sensitive to drops in blood sugar and always have been. There are several reasons for that. The first is poor interoception—we blow past early hunger cues and sometimes forget to eat for long stretches. The second is caffeine; many of us rely on it to function, but it causes blood sugar to dip. And finally, the neurodivergent brain processes and burns through glucose differently—sometimes faster, sometimes less efficiently.

Hypoglycemia feels shaky, confusing, and often quite angry. It makes perfect sense, really—our brains need glucose to function. So when that *"I'm hungry but can't eat"* moment hits, it's not just our wiring at play—it's also that we've run out of fuel.

Over time, Linda has learned to recognize this in me almost immediately. She'll quietly prepare or grab something small that she knows I can tolerate—something simple, easy, familiar—and bring it to me with calm reassurance: *"I know this might not be what you want right now, but let's get something in your belly to bring your blood sugar up. Then we'll figure out what sounds good."* It's perfect. It gives me a clear path forward when my brain can't find one. I don't have to decide, or plan, or think—I just need to eat. That gentle structure, that clarity, makes all the difference.

Then there's the opposite kind of moment—the one that's not about hunger at all, but about restlessness that can't be soothed. It's a peculiar, painful state where I want to do everything and nothing at the same time. My body feels restless, like it needs movement, purpose, or stimulation, but my mind is foggy and uncooperative. Every idea I reach for feels wrong. I'll think, *maybe I should clean something, write something, go for a walk,* but each thought collapses under the weight of indecision and exhaustion. I know if I push myself to move, I'll crash anyway—emotionally, physically, or both—so I stay stuck. It's an unbearable in-between: too restless to rest, too drained to act.

In that state, I start searching for comfort, for something that might ease the internal static. I crave warm, soft, familiar foods—cookies fresh from the oven, mac and cheese, toast with butter—things that promise safety. But no matter what I eat, it never hits the spot. I'm not really hungry; I'm dysregulated. My brain is chasing dopamine, my body is asking for grounding, and my nervous system is sending mixed messages it doesn't know how to interpret.

What I've learned is that this isn't a failure of willpower—it's a physiological and emotional feedback loop. The neurodivergent brain often exists in a heightened state of activation, burning through glucose and neurotransmitters even while sitting still. So when I'm in that restless-but-frozen place, it's not about self-control or discipline; it's about a system that's short-circuiting. The craving for food is just one of the few levers my brain knows to pull in an attempt to self-regulate.

Over time, I've learned to meet these days with more gentleness. Because I generally eat in a way that feels nourishing most of the time, I try to lean into the moments when my system wants comfort and simply allow it.

Sometimes that means cookies or bread or pasta, and I let that be okay. I know my body and brain are asking for something, and even if I can't decode exactly what, I trust that it's part of my process, and I take my comfort wherever I can get it.

I also know for others this cycle can feel more distressing—especially if it happens often or connects to shame around food or body. Wherever we each are in that relationship, it's not a moral issue. It's a reflection of how our systems are wired and the compassion we deserve while navigating that wiring.

Echolalia

Definition: Echolalia is the repetition of words, phrases, or sounds that a person has heard, either immediately after hearing them (immediate echolalia) or after a delay (delayed echolalia). It's a common trait in autism and other forms of neurodivergence and can serve a variety of purposes — including communication, regulation, processing, or expression.

What It Feels Like:

For me, echolalia shows up more internally than externally. I often replay words or phrases in my head—things I've heard in conversation, on TV, or even things I've said. Some people experience this out loud, some internally, and some both. When it does show up more outwardly, it can be challenging mostly because it's misunderstood. Repetition can sound disruptive or random, but it's rarely meaningless. It's just a different form of processing.

Instead of repeatedly asking someone to stop, it's often more helpful to offer a simple accommodation: giving them a quiet space to repeat freely or offering headphones —not necessarily for the person echoing, but for the person who's feeling overwhelmed by the sound. It doesn't need to be a battle. Just a small shift in approach can reduce friction and make room for everyone's wiring to coexist with a little more peace.

Emotional Dysregulation

Definition: Emotional regulation is the ability to recognize, manage, and respond to emotions in a way that feels safe and socially appropriate — both internally and externally. It includes skills like calming yourself when upset, shifting emotional states when needed, expressing feelings in proportion to the situation, and staying connected to yourself and others.

Emotional dysregulation is when emotions become so intense, confusing, or overwhelming that it becomes hard to think clearly, stay grounded, or respond in a way that feels safe or measured. It can look like meltdowns, shutdowns, outbursts, freezing, spiraling thoughts, or intense emotional swings.

For neurodivergent people, emotional regulation can be especially challenging due to differences in nervous system wiring, sensory processing, and communication styles. It's not about being "too emotional" or "immature", it's about how our brains receive, interpret, and respond to emotional input. Emotional regulation is a skill, not a trait, and it *can* be strengthened over time with co-regulation, tools, practice, and understanding. On the flip side, emotional dysregulation—common in neurodivergent individuals—isn't a choice or a character flaw. It's a nervous system response that can be triggered by sensory overload, chronic stress, rejection sensitivity, or the constant mismatch between our internal experience and external demands. When someone is dysregulated, they're not being dramatic, they're weathering an emotional storm without the built-in tools most neurotypical people take for granted.

What it feels like:

Emotional dysregulation is not just "big feelings." It's a full-body, all-systems experience. It can feel like your emotions are hijacking your entire being, drowning in waves you didn't see coming and can't control. For me and my daughter, this kind of dysregulation has been life-shaping. And yet, no one ever explained it to us. I wish more people understood that emotional dysregulation is a neurological trait of neurodivergence. If I had known that earlier, maybe I would have recognized what was happening with Keleigh instead of feeling so lost and ashamed. It would've made such a difference. It baffles me that ADHD diagnoses don't come with a basic rundown of traits. How many of us would have suffered less, or found understanding sooner, if we'd had that missing context?

What Doesn't Work:

Most neurotypical tools for emotional regulation are, for us, trash. Deep breaths, counting to ten, "name it to tame it"—they rarely work. When we try them and *still* spiral, we are left feeling broken, ashamed, or like we're doing it wrong. But we're not. Our emotional volatility is different—stronger, more intense, and wired to move in and out of states unpredictably. We don't build pressure and release it neatly. We surge, shut down, mask, or explode. The timing, the intensity, the recovery—all of it is different. So, tools built for neurotypical regulation often completely miss the mark. When we judge ourselves by how well those tools "should" work, it just adds fuel to the fire.

What Does Work:

Not trying to talk ourselves out of a storm but learning how to ride it. Co-regulation is often more effective than solo strategies: a calm presence, a weighted blanket, a low-demand space, or even just being left alone without judgment. Movement, sensory input, cold water, sound, breath *from the body*, not the brain—all of these are great tools for regulating the nervous system. But most of all, self-compassion. Dysregulation isn't a failure, it's a signal, and it really helps to remind ourselves of that. When we stop trying to be neurotypically calm and instead meet our brains where they are, we can move through dysregulation and out the other side. Rather than attempting to controlling our emotions, it's about supporting ourselves through them.

Accommodations:

- Scheduled downtime: Build in quiet recovery time after overstimulating or emotionally demanding activities (school, work, social events, transitions).
- Sensory supports: Use noise-canceling headphones, weighted blankets, fidgets, calming visuals, or dim lighting to reduce environmental stressors.
- Safe retreat spaces: Designate a calm, low-stimulation area at home or school for regulation breaks.
- Co-regulation: Having a trusted person available who can stay grounded, calm, and present during distress can be crucial—especially for children.
- Use of scripts or visuals: Emotion wheels, charts, or personal coping strategy lists can help externalize internal overwhelm and guide regulation.
- Alternative communication: Allow for written communication, gestures, or even silence during

- dysregulated states. For some, talking makes things worse.
- Flexible expectations: Offer grace during emotional storms. Adjust timing or expectations for conversation, performance, or processing until regulation returns.
- Routine and predictability: Grounding for those prone to emotional swings.
- Movement: Walking, swinging, stretching, or bouncing can help discharge built-up nervous system energy.
- Therapeutic supports: For school or work settings, access to a counselor, school psychologist, or regulation coach can be a vital accommodation.

Radical Acceptance:

For me, radical acceptance of emotional dysregulation means no longer seeing it as a moral failure of mine or my child's. It is a real, neurological experience, not a character flaw or lack of effort. I used to think we just needed to try harder, be calmer, stay in control. Now I know that regulation is a skill, and skills can be taught, supported, and strengthened, but only from a place of safety and understanding. Acceptance doesn't mean giving up on growth. It means meeting ourselves exactly where we are, without shame, and saying: "This is real and hard. And we're doing our best." I still work on improving my emotional regulation, and I support my daughter in doing the same, but we do it with a foundation of compassion, not punishment or pressure. We've learned that progress happens more consistently when we feel safe, not judged.

Executive Dysfunction

Executive Function - Definition: Executive function refers to a set of mental skills that help us manage time, make decisions, control impulses, regulate emotions, plan, shift between tasks, remember instructions, and follow through on goals. It's the brain's command center, the internal manager that helps organize thought, behavior, and action. Executive function allows us to turn intention into action, navigate daily demands, and maintain flexibility when plans change.

Executive Dysfunction - Definition: Executive dysfunction happens when our internal manager isn't functioning well. It's the breakdown of those planning, organizing, and regulating systems. For people with executive dysfunction, even simple tasks like brushing teeth, responding to an email, or starting a project, can feel like trying to plan a mountain climb with no clear path. It's not about being lazy, careless, or unmotivated. It's about a neurological disconnect between *knowing what needs to be done* and *being able to do it*. The intention is there, but the follow-through is blocked.

Adjacent terms:

- **Task initiation paralysis** – particularly related to executive dysfunction, but it deserves a spotlight.
- **Doom piles / clutter blindness** –cleaning and organizing overwhelm due to executive dysfunction and visual processing.
- **Autonomy needs** – The need for control over one's time, space, and decisions.

What it feels like:

Executive dysfunction is, without question, one of the hallmarks of our experience and one of the hardest things to navigate, especially in a society built on productivity, speed, and self-discipline. It's not just inconvenient, it's incredibly painful.

There's a deep, gnawing ache when I know there are things I should be doing, but the connection between knowing and doing is severed. Sometimes I *can* push through with brute force, but it feels like dragging myself through quicksand. It can be physically painful. My thoughts are sluggish, I speak more slowly, I even drive more slowly. It's as if my entire system is underwater, and afterward, I pay a heavy price. I'm left depleted, often needing exorbitant amounts of time to recover.

Living in a world that demands constant hustle and seamless transitions only magnifies this struggle. Deadlines, expectations, social norms—all assume you can just "do the damn thing." But for those of us with executive dysfunction, it's not that simple. One of the hardest parts is how it's perceived. It looks like procrastination, laziness, or indifference, but inside, there's a storm of frustration, shame, and exhaustion. In my experience, 100% of the time it's about ability, not effort. But because it *looks* like effort, people assume I could just try harder—and without a framework for what's happening neurologically, that's the only story that makes sense.

So, I started to believe it too. That I was lazy. That I lacked motivation or discipline. That something was wrong with me.

But learning that executive dysfunction is a neurological difference was life-altering. It allowed me to shift the blame away from my character and instead offer myself compassion. I could finally begin to accommodate my brain's real limits, instead of punishing it for not performing like everyone else's.

One of the most confusing aspects of executive dysfunction is something called uneven productivity. It's when your ability to "do the thing" swings wildly from day to day—or even hour to hour. Some days, it feels like I'm flying. I'm in the zone, unstoppable, crossing off impossible to-do lists, moving mountains. Everything clicks, and it feels effortless.

On those days, my executive functioning is through the roof. Maybe I'm interested in something on my to-do list. Maybe the deadline feels urgent. Maybe the stars align, and my nervous system catches a strange and fleeting surge of energy. Maybe I'm using all the right tools. Maybe some random thing motivates me. Maybe my internal resources are unusually high. Maybe my spoons aren't just available—they're clean, washed, dried, put away, and for some mysterious reason, I have many of them.

For a little while, everything just clicks. And in those moments, I perform and deliver. I move through the world like someone who has it all together. I respond to emails within minutes. I make phone calls without hesitation. I start a task and finish it without walking away halfway through. I cross off to-do list items with an effortless rhythm that feels foreign but exhilarating. I might clean the whole house while I listen to podcasts, cook an elaborate dinner, or finally tackle that mountain of laundry that's been haunting me for weeks. My mind feels sharp. My body cooperative. I'm decisive, efficient, and capable.

I'm completing weeks' worth of work in a single day like I've hacked a secret productivity code.

In the past, that momentum always tricked me. I'd start to believe it: *This is who I really am. The fog has lifted. The blockage is gone. I feel powerful. This is it. It's finally happening. I finally have it together.*

Because I look and feel so capable, I start saying yes to things. I take on projects I can't sustain, make plans I won't have the capacity to follow through on. It feels like I was finally catching up with the rest of the world. But that is an illusion.

I've come to understand that even on the days when it feels effortless, it isn't. I'm sprinting through a marathon. My brain is still running overtime—navigating that tangled highway system in my head—to do what seems simple or automatic for others. On the surface, I may look quick, capable, even efficient. But under the hood, I'm weaving through detours, roundabouts, and mental construction zones just to stay on course. I'm carrying a heavy, invisible weight all the way to the finish line. And when the crash comes, it's brutal.

On those days, I've taken to saying that my executive function is in the trash can—or that I'm having a trash-can day. Any access I previously had to my executive functioning is completely gone. Others might call it ADHD paralysis. It's the full-body shutdown that comes after periods of high output. Even the smallest task feels impossible. I'll sit and stare at what needs to be done, willing myself to start, trying every hack I know, but the bridge between intention and action just isn't there.

It's not procrastination. It's not avoidance. It's a neurological freeze—an actual inability to access executive function. To me, these are the exits in that chaotic highway system of my brain that only appear under certain conditions. And when they don't, no amount of effort or motivation can make them materialize. You can see the destination clearly, but the ramp is gone. There's nowhere to turn, nowhere to go.

On low executive function days, everything feels impossible. I'll sit in front of an open laptop for hours, unable to type a single sentence. I'll stand in the kitchen staring at a sink full of dishes I *know* I need to wash, but I can't seem to move. Time passes strangely—I blink and it's afternoon, and I've done nothing but spiral in my own head. Even things I want to do, things I *care* about, feel like mountains I can't climb. Sometimes I can't even start the microwave. Sometimes I cry over deciding what shirt to wear. The worst part is that I'm always fully aware of everything piling up—but my body won't move. The bridge between thought and action has gone, and I'm stranded on the wrong side.

Sometimes, I feel dead. Not in a dramatic way—just hollow. Like I'm watching life go on from behind glass, completely disconnected from my own momentum. I'm not living, I'm waiting for something in me to come back online. Because I *look* like I'm doing nothing, people assume I *am* doing nothing. But inside, there's gridlock. Every system that helps me move through the world is offline.

More often than not, the shutdown is the direct result of being superhuman the day before. I'm doing more than any one person should be able to do, but for me, it's just my wiring. Those are the days when people see me as a powerhouse—confident, capable, unstoppable. They don't see that I have opposite days too, when I'm frozen on the couch, unable to move for hours.

Other times, the crash doesn't come from visible effort at all, but from the quiet exhaustion of appearing "fine." It's the strain of masking, of holding myself together, of managing the internal chaos so no one else has to. That kind of fatigue builds slowly, invisibly, until my system simply gives out.

And still, I feel guilty.

Whether it's because of how I was raised, or the culture we live in, or some internalized belief I can't quite name, I always think I should be doing more. I *should* be able to push through. I *should* be more productive. That guilt clings to me even when I know better. Even when I understand the neurology. Even when I'm doing all I can. It's a feeling I can't always logic my way out of, and one I quietly carry on the days when I can't carry anything else.

Sometimes, it almost feels like it's all on purpose, or a strange phenomenon I *should* be able to control. Like maybe I *can* be that person I was yesterday all the time. Maybe the problem really is just me, and I've just been making excuses. Success becomes seductive and makes me forget how fragile that access really is. It convinces me I should be able to operate like this all the time, and if I'm not, I must be failing.

But that's the trap. Those bursts of functioning aren't evidence that my struggles aren't real. They're evidence of the complexity and unpredictability of my brain. The on-fire days don't erase the dysfunction. They just make it harder to validate the days when everything shuts down. Because if I did it once, why am I not doing it again?

So people assume I should always be able to. And so do I.

When we know that certain exits only appear when conditions are just right. When they're not there, it's not because I don't care or I'm not trying—it's because the road has shifted. I didn't lose motivation; I lost access. No amount of shame, willpower, or urgency can make an exit appear that isn't there.

When I ignore that truth and force myself to push through, it doesn't just cost me my future executive function. It turns up all the oven knobs. My nervous system spikes. My emotions spiral. I become overwhelmed, volatile, and very often tearful. There's no clarity, just a crash. A wildfire inside me burns everything down in exchange for one checked box.

That is the part no one sees. They see the finished task, the met deadline, the smile on my face. They don't see the hours or days afterward, when I'm curled up, drained and unwell, trying to recover from the toll it took just to *appear* functional.

This is why neurodivergent productivity is so uneven. The good days aren't proof I'm "fixed." They're just the high point in a cycle that inevitably dips. Learning to recognize that cycle without judgment has helped me be gentler with myself. It's helped me find the right language for what's happening.

What doesn't help:

Being told to "just try harder." To make a list. Set a timer. Use a planner. Wake up earlier. Build better habits. Get motivated. I tried *all* of it. I color-coded calendars and never looked at them. I created daily routines I couldn't stick to past the first day. I made to-do lists that became monuments to everything I didn't achieve. I downloaded productivity apps. Read self-help books. Started accountability challenges. I watched YouTube videos from people who seemed to have it all figured out and copied their systems. I journaled, meditated, and wrote affirmations. I prayed. And I shamed myself—quietly but relentlessly—for every failure to follow through.

I thought that if I just tried harder, I could become that productive person I glimpsed every now and then. Those rare on-fire days—maybe once a week, or so, depending on the season of life, seemed like proof that the capacity was *in there*. And if it was in there, surely I could access it. Surely it meant I wasn't trying hard enough the rest of the time. So, I kept pushing. Kept punishing. Kept reaching for structure like it could save me. But none of it got to the real issue because this wasn't about discipline. It wasn't a matter of effort, desire, or willpower. It was about access. It was about the parts of my brain that were never wired to operate on demand. All that trying didn't pull me out of dysfunction, it just buried me deeper in guilt.

What does help:

Understanding how executive dysfunction works. Once I understood that my brain processes task initiation, transitions, and planning differently, I stopped using tools built for neurotypical people and started finding ones that worked for *me*. I let go of rigid planners and productivity hacks that deepened my shame and began experimenting with strategies that honored how my brain naturally functions. Visual cues, body-doubling, gentle momentum starters, flexible lists, and permission to rest became my lifelines. I stopped forcing myself to do it "the normal way" and started building scaffolding around my actual needs.

It wasn't easy. It's taken time and immense work. It's taken a thousand moments of self-interruption and re-patterning to chip away at the deeply ingrained belief that my worth is tied to my output. Sometimes, that old wiring still tries to speak up. But now I have the right framework and tools.

I'll say more about radical acceptance later, but for now I'll just say this: that shift in mindset was the foundation that allowed all of this to take root. Once I stopped trying to fix myself and started supporting myself, everything changed.

Accommodations:

- Break tasks into small, manageable steps. Start tiny to build momentum. Beginning with the hardest thing often sets us up for overwhelm. It can paralyze us before we even get started and, in many cases, leads to the whole to-do list being abandoned. When executive function is a challenge, starting small and building a scaffolding of simple wins is usually far more successful. Our brains benefit from clarity and specificity. For example, instead of writing "clean the kitchen"—which can feel vague and insurmountable—it's often more helpful to list the individual steps: wash the dishes, wipe the counters, sweep the floor, take out the trash. This not only reduces mental friction, but it also allows for a greater sense of progress. Each checked-off step is a tiny burst of momentum. Sometimes that's all we need to keep going.

- Use scaffolding to support task initiation. Scaffolding is the practice of creating external supports or step-by-step structures to help bridge the gap between intention and action. For people with executive dysfunction, it's a way to make a task neurologically accessible when the brain can't yet hold all the pieces at once. Scaffolding breaks the task into manageable, concrete steps, adds cues or routines, and reduces the cognitive load required to begin or sustain effort.

It might look like setting out supplies ahead of time, using visual or auditory reminders, body-doubling with someone else, or simply doing one small action to build momentum. The goal isn't to force productivity—it's to *lower the activation barrier* enough for the brain to gain traction. Scaffolding gives form to what's otherwise invisible, helping us create a pathway where the brain can't yet see one.

An adjacent concept sometimes called Momentum Scaffolding (or *Sequential Activation*) is when one small, accessible action creates the conditions for the next. It's the gentle ignition point that helps the brain bypass the overwhelm of starting. Rather than forcing yourself to begin the "big" task, you begin *somewhere*— anywhere—and allow movement to build naturally.

For example, picking up one piece of trash might lead to putting away a few dishes, then folding laundry, then cleaning the whole room. The process isn't planned—it unfolds as your nervous system finds flow. It's not about discipline; it's about creating traction through motion.

- Use urgency as a tool, not a flaw. For many of us, urgency acts as a neurological switch that activates executive function. I've stopped shaming myself for working best under pressure. Instead, I accept it as part of how my brain works. If waiting until the last minute is what finally helps me access focus and energy, that's okay. Rather than wasting effort trying to force early motivation, I let the timeline do its job—and save my energy for the actual task.

- Add dopamine *before* the task, not after. Play upbeat music, eat a snack, move your body, or do something pleasurable to kickstart action. I like to create a "dopamine menu" for myself—either written down or stored somewhere easy to access—so I don't have to think about what might help in the moment. When my brain starts to spiral and I can't get going, trying to come up with a dopamine boost on the spot is often too much. But if I already have a list, it lowers the barrier. If a loved one has access to that list, they can bring me something from it when I'm stuck—no guessing required.

In a neurotypical world, we're often told we don't deserve a treat until we've completed the task. For a neurodivergent brain that's low on dopamine, a small reward *before* can be what makes the task possible in the first place. This is particularly effective for children. How many times have children been promised a treat *after* a task, only to then freeze, unable to do it? The disappointment and shame they feel when they can't access the action, even though they want to, can be deeply dejecting and traumatizing. They're not refusing or being stubborn. They're stuck. When we reframe the approach—adding dopamine support at the *start*—we set children (and ourselves) up to succeed.

- Gamify tasks. Set timers, make it a challenge, or compete with yourself. Trying to beat a timer is one of my personal favorites. For example, I look at a list of tasks I have and say to myself, I think I can finish all these tasks in 32 minutes and 17 seconds. Next, I set a timer and get to work. This also works for children. Cleaning up becomes "beat the clock" or "how many toys can we put away before the song ends?" Getting ready in the morning turns into "every item you put on earns a silly point," or a race to the finish line with everyone brushing teeth or grabbing shoes at the same time. It's not bribery—it's adding dopamine, momentum, and play to a task that might otherwise feel like a demand. A little fun can bypass a lot of friction.

- Externalize time in ways your brain can recognize. For many of us, time isn't something we feel (see *time blindness*), it's something we need to see in order to manage. That's why tools like visual timers, hourglasses, analog clocks, calendars, and alarms aren't just organizational aids—they're essential replacements for an internal sense of time that may not exist. Digital countdowns, color-coded schedules, or even physically moving sticky notes across a timeline can make time more real and more manageable. These strategies are accommodations that help bridge the gap between time as it's expected to work, and time as we actually experience it.

- Leverage interest and novelty. Our systems tend to be interest-based, so if something is interesting, it's easier to access our executive functioning. When possible, let yourself follow the energy.

A great example of this is with children who struggle with executive function around cleaning their teeth. To keep it interesting, I've bought all kinds of toothbrushes—different colors, children themed, adult-themed, electric, old-school, ones that light up, ones connected to apps. We've tried every toothpaste flavor known to man—sparkle unicorn, watermelon, cinnamon, bubblegum—and rotated mouthwashes, xylitol gum, whatever worked. It's a phenomenal way to *avoid a power struggle*, and instead honor the child's system. The goal isn't to "enforce compliance," it's to get their teeth brushed without constant fighting, arguing, or bribing.

Another example is showering or bathing—something many people struggle with due to executive function. So again, we make it interesting. My children used to take baths while watching TV on an iPad. We rotated new loofahs, fun body wash, bath markers, different kinds of shampoo and conditioner—even glitter, if that's what it took. The point wasn't luxury—it was access. It was honoring what their system needed to get over the activation wall.

This works for adults too. Wherever I can, I still add interest when a task is hard for my executive function. New dish soap. My favorite music. A pretty notebook. A weird mug. We don't have to suffer our way through everything. Sometimes all we need is a little dopamine and permission to make it fun.

For younger children especially, novelty often wears off quickly, so if something stops working, I just tuck it away in a bin and bring it back in a month. Add new things as needed. It doesn't have to be wasteful—anyone else in the house can use the extras. I've even gotten fun beach towels at Goodwill just to spark interest. A good thrift session can help us find something we like without the added toll on the environment or our pocket.

- Reimagine your to-do list. Eliminate unnecessary tasks (even things that feel required), and rethink *how* things get done. Efficiency isn't always linear.

This might seem like an odd thing to include, but I think it belongs here. About six years ago, I stopped using traditional soap and stopped showering in the conventional sense. I found the daily routine of showering and "getting ready" draining, overwhelming, and unsustainable. Then I learned about Ayurvedic approaches to cleansing, and it immediately made sense to my body and brain.

Instead of forcing myself through a standard hygiene routine, I built one that works for me. I take detox baths, I dry brush, I use self-massage and natural exfoliants. I rotate different oils, herbs, clays, and elements that feel good for my skin and nervous system. And I haven't suffered a single harmful side effect. In fact, I feel healthier, calmer, and more at home in my own body.

It's a perfect example of how something that feels impossible—like daily showering—doesn't *have* to be done the way we were taught. When I moved the goalpost and reimagined the task, I found an alternative that worked. Sometimes that's the key:

challenging even the "must-dos" and asking, *is there a way to meet this need that honors my system instead of punishing it?*

Laundry is another example of something that can be completely reimagined. If the pile never ends and just looking at it makes your chest tighten, maybe it's not about trying harder. Maybe it's time to change the rules. Maybe you only wash towels once a week. Maybe jeans and pajamas get worn multiple times before they hit the basket. Maybe you toss clothes in the dryer with a splash of vinegar and a few ice cubes to freshen them instead of running a full wash. Maybe you build a wardrobe with enough basics to last a week and do one big laundromat trip in an hour, instead of doing a little every day. Maybe you trade the task with someone else in your home or outsource it if finances allow. The point is that *trying and failing over and over isn't functional*. It doesn't build skills, it builds shame. And shame doesn't help anyone fold a damn thing.

- Change the narrative around task completion. You don't have to do things "the right way"—you just have to do them *your* way. Give yourself permission to redefine success: messy, imperfect, late, or segmented is still done. Focus on *completion*, not perfection. Another laundry example: when I had a house full of kids, laundry was my arch nemesis. The towels were kept in a cabinet, and at some point I just stopped folding them. I just threw them straight from the clean basket into the cabinet. Who cares if your towel is folded? It just needs to be clean (or in this case even kind of clean was good enough most days). This mindset shift can lower the activation energy needed to get started and ease the internal pressure that so often leads to paralysis.

- On low-functioning days, delegate or ask for help. Not every day will be a high-capacity day—and that's okay. On days when executive function feels completely offline, lean on your support. That might mean asking your partner to talk you through your to-do list, handing off a chore, or even just saying, "I'm not functioning well today, can you help me prioritize?" Or even better yet? "Can you help me figure out what can be put off for today and get done at a later time?" Sharing the load isn't weakness, it's wisdom. It protects your energy and helps prevent burnout.

- Use body-doubling to initiate and sustain attention. Sometimes just having another person nearby can help spark your brain into motion and is especially effective for task initiation. The presence of another regulated nervous system offers co-regulation and accountability without pressure. You don't even need to be doing the same task—just not being alone in the struggle can provide an internal shift. Added note: for some neurodivergent folks the opposite can be true, we can better access our executive function when everyone leaves and we are left to not be perceived in any way. Side note to the added note: Sometimes both can be true at different times.

- Rely on visual supports and reminders. Sticky notes, phone alerts, whiteboards, and labeled spaces are all tried-and-tested ways that help get things done. One of my favorite executive function hacks is using the maps app on my phone *while I'm getting ready*. I enter the exact location I need to be, and it shows me what time I'd arrive *if I left right now*—no backwards time math required. It keeps me on track visually without having to hold all those calculations in my head.

Set phone alarms for everything (and name them). I use alarms constantly, and sometimes I set *multiple* alarms for the same task—because I know one won't always be enough. I've set one alarm to remind me of something, and then two or three more alarms to remind me again just in case I forget after the first one. I've had alarms set at different points in the morning to help me stay aware of how much time I have left, what still needs to happen, what I should be finishing. Trash goes out on a Tuesday, so I have multiple alarms on Monday as reminders. I've had alarms to remind me to pick up my children as well as alarms to *take* my children. I use alarms for basic and important things because I've learned not to assume I'll remember anything. Not even my children. Instead of feeling bad about that, I just set an alarm. That's the system. That's the support. That's what works.

- Create routines with spaciousness. Build in transition time and buffer zones between tasks. Stacking tasks back-to-back sounds efficient, but for many of us, it leads straight to overwhelm. Instead, routines that leave breathing room allow us to shift gears more gently and avoid cognitive overload. Ten minutes between tasks might be the difference between melting down and moving forward. That space *is* part of the routine—it's not wasted time, it's what makes the rest of it possible.

- Use "start rituals" to ease into action. Starting is often the hardest part. Connecting a specific ritual—music, lighting a candle, putting on shoes, pulling back your hair, turning on a lamp—to the act of beginning can signal to your brain: *it's time.* These rituals build a bridge between stillness and motion, helping us shift more smoothly into action without the shock of abrupt demands.

- Allow movement breaks and sensory regulation moments. We're not robots. Our nervous systems need tending. Whether it's stretching, stepping outside, rocking in a chair, using a fidget, or rubbing lotion into your hands—these regulation pauses make a huge difference. They give the brain a moment to reset, recalibrate, and come back online so that focus and productivity aren't being forced through a dysregulated state.

- Permit nontraditional work rhythms. Honor energy spikes that can happen at unconventional times. Many of us have sleep–wake cycles that don't follow the standard mold. Our melatonin release may be delayed or mistimed, which means our most productive hours might not match what the world considers a "normal" schedule. And that's okay.

For me, my most productive stretch of the day is between 5 a.m. and about 9 or 10 a.m., depending on the day. That's when my brain is most alive, when tasks feel doable, and when I've learned to knock out the things that matter most. So, I save things for that span of time. I don't stress about what "should" get done in the afternoon or evening—I just plan to do it at 5 a.m.

And most of the time, I do. Because I wake up early and move through my day in that flow, I'm often *done* by mid-afternoon. After lunch, I know I won't be productive, so I don't expect myself to be. I've stopped trying to force focus or push through. And I go to bed really early. It's not conventional. But it works.

For others, that energy spike might come at 10 p.m., or even 2 a.m. Nighttime can be a period of intense clarity, momentum, and flow. Some people only find their brain "turns on" once the world quiets down—when the pressure has gone and the sensory input lowers. If that's when the magic happens, that's when it happens. The key is to give ourselves permission to notice those patterns and honor them.

Before I started honoring my rhythm, I used to spend every afternoon and evening trying to catch up—forcing myself to "get it together" and finish the day "right." But it was always a losing battle. I ended up overwhelmed, overstimulated, and crying almost every night. My relationships suffered, and my nervous system was fried. Eventually, I crashed into full-on burnout.

I also used to sort of *pass out* every night—not in a gentle, restful way, but in a full-body shutdown. My brain and body would just give out. Often, I wouldn't even realize it was coming until I was already slipping under. Sometimes I'd feel a wave of panic and urgency—like I had to lie down *immediately*—but by the time I laid down, I'd already be gone. In the moments leading up to it, I was frantic, wild even, moving on autopilot in a kind of dissociative trance. I rarely remembered anything that happened just before it happened. Looking back, I can clearly see that it was my system force-quitting after too many hours of override. I had been pushing past my limits for so long that my body finally, and without subtlety, took the wheel.

Now I know that honoring my natural rhythm isn't lazy or indulgent. It's survival. It's sustainability. It's what lets me function without constantly collapsing. There's no single right way to structure a day. The right way is the one that works for you—even if that means rewriting every rule about when productivity is supposed to happen.

- Reduce task-switching demands. Minimize interruptions and context changes.
  For neurodivergent brains, every shift from one task to another—even something small like checking a message mid-project—can create a disproportionate amount of mental friction. It's not about being inflexible, it's about the cost of reorienting. Reducing unnecessary switches helps preserve energy and keep focus intact. This might mean batching similar tasks together, setting boundaries around interruptions, or finishing one thing before beginning another.

- Avoid multitasking. Single-tasking is usually more accessible and sustainable. While multitasking is often praised, for those of us with executive function challenges, it's usually a recipe for burnout. Switching back and forth between tasks fragments attention and exhausts mental resources. Single-tasking—fully engaging in one thing at a time—can feel slower, but it is almost always more effective and less stressful in the long run. Giving your full focus to one task at a time respects how your brain works best.

- Try a short, timed sprint. Sometimes, when nothing else is working—when your room's a disaster, the house feels like too much, and your executive function has flatlined for the day—it helps to shrink the task. Set a timer for just a few minutes and see how much you can get done. It doesn't have to be six minutes, though that's one of my go-tos. It can be three minutes. Or ten. Or thirteen minutes and twenty-six seconds, if that's what your brain likes. Pick a number that feels non-threatening, set the timer, and just go. You don't have to finish everything—just do *something*.

    It's not about perfection. You'll often be surprised by how much you can do in that small window—not just for your space, but for your nervous system. If you live with other people, get them involved. Three or four people cleaning like mad for a few minutes can reset the energy of a room.

    You can name it the Six Minute Scramble, or something else fun depending on the timer length (Ten-Minute Tornado, anyone?). Make it a race, blast a song, assign silly points. After that, rest. You may find that what felt impossible before now feels... doable.

- Normalize crash recovery. Acknowledge that after high-output times, rest isn't optional, it's essential. Sometimes, it takes longer than we think it *should*, which can feel frustrating—especially when we've already rested. I've had so many days where I think, *"But I rested all day yesterday, I should feel better today."* But the truth is, our systems don't run or respond on a 24-hour reset timer. It doesn't mean we're doing something wrong; it just means recovery is still happening.

For neurodivergent folks, high-output times often mean we were running on adrenaline, masking, or pushing beyond what our bodies and brains could handle. The crash afterward isn't failure, it's fallout, and it may not resolve in a single evening of rest. Sometimes it takes one day. Sometimes it takes three. Sometimes we rest for two days and still feel like we got hit by a truck.

The sooner we stop resisting the crash and start honoring it, the less shame we carry. The less shame we carry, the more space we create for meaningful repair. The more we acknowledge our need for rest—without judgment or guilt—the faster our systems can reset. You don't have to quickly bounce back, you just have to listen. Trust that honoring your limits is not what's slowing you down—it's what allows you to keep going.

- Accept that executive function fluctuates. Design systems with flexibility, not rigidity. Consistency is often held up as the gold standard, but for neurodivergent people, fluidity is often a more compassionate and realistic goal. Remember: the same strategy won't work every time. What helps one day, might fall flat the next. There will be days when you try several different tools, and nothing clicks. That doesn't mean you're broken or doing it wrong—it means your system is asking for something different. Sometimes, that something is rest. When the tools stop working, that's often a sign to pause, honor your mind and body, and revisit the task later. Flexibility is not failure. Building an adaptable support system is just as important as having one that works.

These accommodations aren't shortcuts. They're bridges—built by us, for us—within our life that feels more possible and authentic.

Radical Acceptance:

Even the best tools in the world won't help if you're trapped in a silent battle with yourself. For a long time, I was. I kept thinking that I just needed to try harder, be better, and push through. I thought I was failing because I couldn't do things the way others could.

Radical acceptance didn't come to me as a lightning bolt. Instead, it came in quiet moments of exhaustion, in the aftermath of yet again a series of fire days.

This kind of acceptance isn't about giving up. It's about laying down the weapons we use against ourselves and saying, "Okay. This is who I am. This is how my brain works, and I'm done apologizing for it." It's the shift from constantly trying to fix myself, to gently learning how to care for myself. Not when I've earned it, or when I've checked enough boxes. But now.

That means letting go of the shame that tells me I should do more, or that rest is only deserved after a hard day's work. That I must do life like everyone else for it to count.

Radical acceptance sounds like this:
"This is just how my brain works."
"There's nothing wrong with me for needing support."

"My ways of doing things are valid, even if no one else understands them."

It also means accepting that I might never be "consistent" in the way people expect.
I'll probably always need external reminders, alarms, and scaffolding. Some days will be smooth, and others will be complete chaos. Rest isn't optional, it's essential—and I don't have to earn it.

The hardest part? Turning down the volume on that voice in my head that says:
"You should be able to do this."
"You're just being dramatic."
"You should've figured this out by now."

That voice is the echo of a world that doesn't understand how much energy it takes for some of us to participate in life. The more I recognize that voice, the less power it has over me.

What's even more powerful is this: when I change the way I talk to myself—when I soften the internal narrative—I start to change the way I speak out loud. I name what's really happening. I say, "My executive function is in the trash can today. I need to rest and see how I feel in a little bit." And that clarity shifts everything. It changes how others respond to me. It can even change how *they* speak to themselves. And for Keleigh, that shift in language isn't just helpful, it's healing. When Keleigh hears me name my needs and honor my brain, it gives her a new script. A better story. One that says, "I'm not bad. I'm not lazy. I just need support." That's the gift of radical acceptance: it doesn't end with us. It ripples outward and rewrites the narrative for the people we love most.

I don't need to "overcome" my brain, I just need to work with it. When I do that—when I stop fighting myself—there's space for rest, joy, and helpful systems. For the kind of life that doesn't just look functional on the outside, but feels good on the inside. That's peace and freedom. That's the real beginning of everything.

Invisible Disability Paradox

For many neurodivergent women—especially those who present as conventionally "put together" or "normal"—there's a painful paradox we live in every day. Our appearance, tone, smile, or even just our ability to make eye contact, can create the illusion that we're neurotypical. That illusion sometimes protects us, but it can also be isolating. Under the surface, we are often struggling in unseen ways.

Because of how I look, people often assume I should be able to effortlessly perform social norms. That I should be comfortable with small talk, respond the "right" way, and roll with social norms. But I often miss cues and freeze in conversations. I say the wrong thing or nothing at all. When that happens, it's often met not with compassion, but with confusion, judgment, or even hostility. People don't see my neurodivergence, they just see a sudden break in my performance—and they interpret that as rudeness, moodiness, or just being difficult.

This gap between how I look and how I function can feel like a trap. There's an unspoken contract: *You look normal, so you'd better act normal too*. When I can't meet that expectation, people often feel let down or even threatened. I've experienced harsh judgment because of this mismatch — and even more painfully, I've internalized it and believed that I was the problem.

When your internal experience is invisible but intense, and your outer presentation says, "I'm fine," you begin to question your own reality. You start to mask harder. You fawn. You shrink. And the grief of being misunderstood—*consistently* misunderstood—cuts deep.

Understanding this paradox has given me language. It's not my fault that I'm misread. It's not because I'm faking or trying to confuse people. It's because my disability is invisible, and I've spent a lifetime trying to survive the dissonance between how I feel and how I'm perceived.

Interest-Based Systems

Definition: An interest-based system refers to the way many neurodivergent individuals are naturally wired to focus, engage, and act *based on interest*, rather than external rewards, consequences, or expectations. This means that motivation, task initiation, and sustained attention are often closely tied to whether something is stimulating, meaningful, or personally relevant—not just whether it's "important" or has a deadline.

What It Feels Like:

What it feels like is usually horrible, because our world is designed for people who can "just do the thing." But for those of us with interest-based nervous systems, it doesn't work like that. If something isn't interesting, engaging, or emotionally relevant, it can feel almost *physically impossible* to do—no matter how important it is. Meanwhile, when something new, shiny, or personally meaningful pops up, our system instantly kicks into gear without hesitation. That contrast can be gutting.

Here's a perfect example: When I was just coming out of deep burnout, Linda asked me to do her a huge favor. She had agreed to take an old acquaintance to surgery in a neighboring state, but she got called into work at the last minute. She asked if I could go instead—a four-to-five-hour drive, waiting at the hospital, maybe staying overnight. At that point, she was working full time and supporting me completely, and I didn't have any big obligations. But I just couldn't make my system agree to doing it. I felt awful, and so did Linda.

The next day, I found out someone I *adore* was doing a tour and would be holding an event in a different neighboring state. Instantly, I was like, *see you later,* and drove five hours without a second thought. I had the energy, drive, and alignment. But it came with a huge wave of guilt. Why couldn't I show up for Linda when it mattered?

That's the trap of interest-based motivation: it doesn't mean we don't care — it means our systems literally don't ignite without the spark. The engine won't turn over, no matter how much logic, guilt, or urgency we pour into it.

That example was a big one, but I experience it in a million tiny ways too — like the time I couldn't find the interest to file my taxes for three years (okay, that's a pretty big one too). On a smaller, everyday level, it's why so many of us have a long list of "adult" tasks waiting — phone calls to make, forms to fill out, things that *should* get done — but then suddenly we're deep in a craft project or reorganizing the tool drawer. It's not avoidance; it's just where the spark showed up.

Just yesterday, I had an outdoor task that's been on my to-do list for months. And of course, my system decided the *coldest, snowiest* day of the year would be the perfect time for interest to appear. It's not a choice — it just happens that way. And honestly, most of the time, even *we're* not happy about it.

What doesn't help:

What doesn't help is shame—our own or from others. Being told we should just push through, try harder, or be more disciplined doesn't magically unlock the motivation switch. It just makes us feel broken, lazy, or flawed. External pressure without internal connection—like deadlines, guilt-tripping, or even reward systems—often backfires. Neurotypical methods like to-do lists or "treats when you finish" don't usually work for brains that can't access the task without genuine engagement. When people tie our worth to productivity, or act like we're failing on purpose, it erodes self-trust and deepens the paralysis. Being forced to do boring or draining things without flexibility can shut us down completely or push us into burnout. One of the most painful misunderstandings is when people think we *won't* do something — when in reality, we *can't*.

What does help: Understanding how our brains actually work, and working *with* that wiring instead of against it. Interest isn't just a preference for us; it's a neurological ignition switch. To help build momentum, when possible, lean into what's engaging or meaningful. Starting with the fun part of a task, finding ways to tie it to something we care about, or reframing it in a way that sparks curiosity, can make a huge difference. Body doubling (doing tasks alongside someone else), timers, novelty, and gentle structure can also help us access hard-to-reach tasks. Most of all, having compassion for ourselves—and being around people who *get it*— allows us to shift from blame to strategy. It's not about avoiding responsibility; it's about building systems that work for our brains. When we stop wasting energy trying to be neurotypical, we have more capacity to do the things that matter, on our terms.

Accommodations:

- Body doubling: Working alongside someone else (virtually or in person) to help activate task initiation.
- Start with the fun part: Give permission to skip the "logical order" and begin with whatever is most engaging or accessible.
- Reframe the task: To create internal relevance, connect the task to a personal value, special interest, or long-term goal.
- Use novelty to your advantage: New locations, tools, playlists, or approaches can help break through task inertia.
- Gamify it: Turning tasks into a game, challenge, or timed mission can sometimes tap into dopamine pathways.
- Use visual reminders or checklists: This is not to force the task, but to externalize what's otherwise floating around internally.
- Build in recovery time: Recognize the effort required for uninteresting tasks and allow downtime afterward.

- Flexible scheduling: Allow windows of time instead of rigid deadlines, so tasks can align with natural motivation peaks.
- Remove moral judgment: Create an environment where doing something *later* or *differently* isn't treated as failure.
- Support from others: Having someone who can help break down, scaffold, or even *co-do* a task can be essential—not a weakness.

Radical Acceptance:

For me, radical acceptance has meant letting go of guilt. I used to think I was just lazy or selfish, especially when I could somehow pull off amazing feats for something I *wanted* to do, but not for things I "should" do. It felt awful. But I've come to understand that interest lights up my system and gives me access to energy, focus, and action. When that interest isn't there, it's like trying to start a car with no gas. Now I try to build my life around how my brain functions, instead of fighting it. I have responsibilities, but I approach them with tools, flexibility, and kindness. And when I *can't* do something, I don't spiral into shame. I name it, use accommodations or ask for help, and pivot. This isn't a moral failure. It's just a different operating system. The more I honor that, the more I thrive.

Interoception

Definition: Our brain's ability to sense, interpret, and respond to signals from inside our body— things like hunger, thirst, pain, temperature, fatigue, the need to use the bathroom, and even emotions. It's often called the "eighth sense," and it plays a crucial role in self-awareness, regulation, and well-being.

For many neurodivergent people, interoception is disrupted. This means we may not notice or correctly interpret what our bodies are trying to tell us, or we might notice too much, too late, or in a way that's confusing.

Examples of interoception challenges:

- Not knowing you're hungry until you're shaky or angry ("hangry" and/or hypoglycemic)
- Struggling to tell the difference between hunger and anxiety
- Not realizing you need to use the bathroom until it's urgent
- Not feeling thirst until you have a headache or feel dizzy
- Getting overheated or freezing without registering it until you're already distressed
- Difficulty identifying emotions because you can't read physical signals (tight chest, racing heart, nausea, etc.)
- Not noticing fatigue until you completely crash
- Being told to "listen to your body" and wondering how

What it feels like:

One of my funniest (and most awkward) experiences of interoception mismatch happened at a somatic breath workshop. It was an intense two-hour session: dim lights, loud music, deep breathing, and the people around me were having spiritual breakdowns or breakthroughs — sobbing, shaking, releasing decades of trauma. At the end, the instructor asked us to journal what had come up for us. I had, of course, forgotten a notebook, so I borrowed a scrap of paper and a pen. Around the room, people were tearfully sharing how they'd connected with their inner child, unearthed forgotten grief, or felt emotional blockages physically move through their body. When I glanced down at my paper, all I had written was: *"I need to drink more green tea."* That was it. Not a single repressed memory or cosmic realization—just a beverage note. I quietly folded the paper, returned the pen, and made a fast exit.

For me, that was interoception. My body was trying to tell me something—just not what everyone else's bodies seemed to be shouting. And that's the point. Interoception in neurodivergent folk can show up in unusual ways. We may not always know when we're hungry, tired, or anxious, but sometimes, in a quiet moment of breath work, we suddenly know we need antioxidants. So, the happy ending was that I did start drinking more green tea. Maybe my nervous system *did* get what it needed, after all.

I've been able to make some improvements, but just a teeny tiny bit, and it's taken a *shit ton* of conscious effort. I've learned to check in with my body — to pause and ask basic questions like, "Am I hungry?", "Do I need to pee?", or "Could this tight chest be anxiety?" It's not intuitive, but I've built a little more awareness. And even that small amount of progress has made a big difference.

It's like learning to speak a language I was never taught — I'll probably always have an accent, but at least now I can ask "How are you?" and "Where is the restroom?" Two very important things to know.

Accommodations:

- Create structured body check-in routines. Build in daily pauses to ask "Am I hungry? Thirsty? Tired? Needing a break?" If helpful, use visual prompts or body maps.
- Encourage preemptive bathroom routines. Prompt children (and remind yourself) to use the bathroom at regular transition points (before school, before leaving the house, before bed), *even if they don't feel the urge*, because their body's internal signals might come too late.
- Use external cues for internal needs. Timers, schedules, or habit trackers can help regulate eating, hydration, sleep, and bathroom breaks.
- Normalize conversations about bodily signals. Say things like "My stomach feels kind of funny—maybe I need a snack" to model interpreting internal cues out loud.
- Offer co-regulation for body awareness. Gently guide through identifying sensations: "Your face looks tense—do you think you might be feeling frustrated or hot?"
- Use clothing and environmental clues. Cold hands might mean a need for a jacket. A pale face could mean hunger. Help identify external signs when internal ones are unreliable.
- Support emotional interoception. Label emotions as they show up: "It seems like you're getting really quiet—do you think you're feeling overwhelmed or tired?"
- Encourage somatic tools. Gentle movement, stretching, body scans, and breathing exercises can help reconnect with internal signals.
- Honor differences without shame. Recognize that interoception varies widely. Struggling with it doesn't

mean someone is "out of touch," it just means their wiring works differently.

Lack of Intuitive Social Processing

Definition: Lack of intuitive social processing refers to the difficulty or inability to automatically interpret, respond to, or predict social cues and norms in real time. This includes challenges with things like reading facial expressions, body language, tone of voice, implied meanings, and unspoken social rules—all of which neurotypical individuals tend to process instinctively or subconsciously.

What it feels like:

It's hard to explain just how disorienting the world is without intuitive social processing, without automatically understanding what people mean, how they feel, or what's expected in a social moment. For me, it felt like a constant state of confusion in almost every relationship. I didn't realize other people weren't that confused. I thought no one really understood what was going on, that it must have been what all relationships were like. I thought everyone was silently guessing and second-guessing like I was. It wasn't until much later that I learned most people pick up on social information that I don't—facial expressions, power plays, hidden meanings. I was trying to play a game when no one told me the rules.

My marriage experienced an ongoing and difficult time and one day, I broke down sobbing and cried out, "I'm just so confused!" It wasn't just about that disagreement — it was about everything. A lifetime of misreading people, misplacing trust, and feeling like I was always one step behind in conversations, friendships, and love. That confusion has caused me so much grief. Until I understood my neurodivergence, I didn't believe it was a personal failing, because I didn't even know I was failing. I had no awareness that other people weren't operating with the same level of difficulty. I just thought that life felt murky, unpredictable, and slightly off for everyone, and that maybe I just needed to try harder.

A Note on Vulnerability and Potential for Unhealthy Relationships

This confusion—this lack of intuitive social processing—doesn't just make relationships harder. It can also make us more vulnerable to manipulation and abuse. Many neurodivergent people, me included, struggle to read red flags. We often take things literally, think people mean what they say, and assume the best in others. We may not notice when someone is crossing a line, gaslighting us, or subtly controlling the situation. We often miss the subtext because we're focused on the content. And in that gap between what's said and what's meant, unhealthy dynamics can grow.

I didn't see the power plays, the emotional bait-and-switch, or the slow erosion of trust in myself. I just kept trying harder to please, accommodate, and keep the peace. Fawning and people-pleasing are often part of the neurodivergent experience, especially when we've been taught to mask to fit in. Predators, whether they know it consciously or not, can sense that vulnerability.

Accommodations:

- Direct, clear communication. Avoid sarcasm, vague implications, or social "games." Say what you mean
- Written follow-ups to conversations, tasks, or expectations (especially after meetings or emotionally charged discussions)
- Permission to ask clarifying questions without judgment—this includes pausing to say, "Can you rephrase that?" or "I'm not sure what that meant"
- Time to process social situations. Allow space after interactions to debrief or reflect, instead of expecting immediate reactions
- Gentle correction or guidance without shaming when social cues are missed. For example, "That came across a little blunt, even if that wasn't your intention"
- Role-play or modeling of common social situations in safe spaces (helpful in therapy, coaching, or family environments)
- Extra support in new group settings, such as a peer buddy, social script, or pre-event briefing about dynamics or expectations
- Avoidance of high-stakes group interactions without support, like unstructured meetings, public introductions, or intense group discussions
- Encouragement to express needs directly, rather than waiting for the person to pick up on unspoken cues
- Respect for different communication styles, including slower processing time or need for written responses over verbal ones
- Validation that confusion is real and valid—not a flaw, but a processing difference
- Opportunities to process social situations with a trusted person afterward, especially when something felt "off" but the person isn't sure why

- Training or coaching for neurotypical peers, coworkers, or teachers, so they understand this trait and can respond with empathy instead of irritation

Late Diagnosis / Misdiagnosis

For many neurodivergent people—especially women and AFAB individuals—the road to understanding is long, winding, and often littered with detours. Being missed, misunderstood, or mislabeled can carry quiet devastation. We grow up feeling "off" but never quite know why. We're told we're too sensitive, dramatic, spacey, intense, or simply too much, so we internalize it. When we do seek help, we're often misdiagnosed with anxiety, depression, bipolar disorder, borderline personality disorder, or even told nothing is wrong at all.

It's not that boys and men aren't deeply impacted by late or misdiagnosis—they absolutely are—but the gendered masking and social expectations placed on girls and women make it harder to see. We're praised for compliance, people-pleasing, and working twice as hard to get half as far. Meanwhile, our actual neurodivergence is buried under layers of coping and camouflage.

One of the most common (and painful) patterns is that diagnosis often comes only after a system collapse—especially in motherhood. The scaffolding we built to survive begins to fall apart under the relentless demands of parenting. What once passed for "functional" becomes impossible. Routines crumble, emotional regulation vanishes, and all the cracks we spent decades patching up start to rupture.

Other times, the unraveling begins not with ourselves, but with our children. A mom starts trying to get support for her struggling child and, somewhere along the way, recognizes herself in every book, article, and evaluation form. It's like holding up a mirror. That realization can be profoundly healing, but also heartbreaking. We begin to understand just how many years were spent in confusion, self-blame, or quiet suffering.

Late diagnosis brings relief, but it also brings grief for what we endured without language. Grief for the support we didn't receive. Grief for the ways we misunderstood ourselves and were misunderstood by others. But from that grief can come clarity, community, and self-compassion.

Accommodations here are emotional as much as practical: space to process the grief, access to affirming neurodivergent-led spaces, and support in unmasking, rebuilding, and redefining what life can look like—no longer with the shame and survival scripts.

Two related terms to know:

Internalized Ableism – When you've spent a lifetime being misunderstood, dismissed, or told you're "too much" or "not trying hard enough," you start to believe it. Internalized ableism is the shame we carry from those experiences—the quiet voice that says we *should* be able to function like everyone else. It runs deep, and often without our awareness, so it can be hard to accept support or even see ourselves as neurodivergent.

Cycle of Over functioning and Collapse – Many late-diagnosed or high-masking adults live in a constant pattern of pushing themselves past capacity, then crashing hard. We over-function— often out of necessity or conditioning—until our systems can't take any more. Then we collapse for days, weeks, or even months. It's a brutal cycle that can only shift when we recognize it, name it, and begin to live in ways that honor our actual capacity.

Masking & Camouflaging

Definition: Masking is the conscious or unconscious act of hiding, minimizing, or overriding one's natural neurodivergent traits in order to fit into neurotypical expectations. This can include suppressing stimming, forcing eye contact, copying social cues, hiding overwhelm or confusion, scripting conversations, or pretending to understand when you don't. Camouflaging is closely related and often refers more specifically to blending in by mimicking others, adopting personas, or masking autistic traits in social situations.

Masking and camouflaging are not about deception—they are survival strategies.

They develop early, often unconsciously, as a response to rejection, ridicule, punishment, or persistent misattunement. Over time, they become so ingrained that many of us don't realize we're doing it. It's not something we *choose*, it's something we *become* in order to navigate a world that doesn't feel safe for our true selves.

What It Feels Like:

Masking isn't about pretending to be someone you're not — it's about surviving in a world that doesn't make room for who you are. There are really two kinds of masking for me — the non-deliberate kind that happens automatically, like breathing, and the deliberate kind I've learned through years of observation.

The automatic version is pure reflex. My brain scans for cues, reads the room, adjusts tone, mirrors body language, calculates timing, and decides what version of me feels safest to bring forward. Often, by the time I even realize it's happening, it's already done.

The deliberate version is different — it's intentional, practiced, and constantly refined. It shows up in small physical adjustments: laughing when others laugh, turning my knees and toes straight ahead so my gait looks "normal," holding my arms in a tight ninety-degree angle when I run with my hands in a loose fist. Tiny acts designed to help me blend in. They're not big or dramatic, but they're carefully monitored, like a background program running in my brain — social camouflage operating moment by moment.

The non-deliberate masking is so subconscious that I rarely notice myself doing the observing part — the subtle data-gathering, the constant calibrating. I only recognize it afterward, through the clues it leaves behind. Sometimes I replay an interaction and wonder why I agreed with something I didn't actually believe, or why my speech pattern shifted mid-conversation, or why I slipped into an old memorized script. Other times, I don't analyze it at all — I just feel bone-tired, disconnected, or unsure what really happened. Those moments of confusion and exhaustion are often the only evidence that I've been masking.

And yet, it's complicated. Masking doesn't always feel bad. Sometimes it feels *good*. Safe. Familiar. There's comfort in knowing the role, in having a script that keeps me from stumbling or being misunderstood. In those moments, the mask itself can feel soothing — like a well-worn blanket that wraps around me in social uncertainty.

Recently, I've been exploring something in therapy that changed how I see it: sometimes the masked parts of me are still *me*. They're not false — they're just adapted. The warmth, humor, competence, and calm I project are all real. They just exist inside a carefully managed framework. I used to think masking made me fake, but now I see that even when I'm masked, I'm still real. It's just a version of me that learned how to survive.

The exhaustion comes later — the deep, cellular fatigue from holding that framework in place for too long. It's not weakness; it's the crash that comes after hours (or decades) of performance-level self-monitoring.

How It Shows Up:

- Smiling or nodding even when confused, upset, or overwhelmed
- Mimicking others' body language, tone, or speech patterns to blend in
- Suppressing stimming or sensory needs
- Avoiding honesty about needs, boundaries, or confusion
- Forcing eye contact or practicing facial expressions in the mirror
- Pre-writing texts or scripting conversations

- Changing clothing, tone, or mannerisms based on the group
- Performing competence in school, parenting, work, or social settings—then collapsing in private
- Saying "I'm fine" when you're not, because explaining feels riskier than hiding

Long-Term Impact:

Masking can be deeply adaptive — sometimes it's the only way to move through a world that isn't built for our wiring. It can protect us, help us connect, and allow us to function in spaces that might otherwise feel inaccessible. But it also carries a cost. Over time, the energy it takes to maintain that adaptation can lead to exhaustion, burnout, and a quiet kind of disconnection from ourselves.

For some of us, it shows up as losing track of who we are beneath all the versions we've learned to perform. For others, it looks like living in constant tension — torn between safety and self-expression. The longer we rely on the mask without space to rest or unmask, the heavier it becomes.

But it's not all harm. With self-understanding, support, and safe environments, we can learn to find balance with our masks — to wear them consciously when needed, and to take them off when it's safe. Masking isn't inherently wrong; it's a tool we developed for survival. There's no single right approach. Each of us has to find our own balance between safety and authenticity, and that balance can shift depending on the moment.

What matters most is understanding ourselves — and using that understanding to make the best decisions for our own wellbeing, moment by moment.

Accommodations:

- Normalize unmasking in safe spaces—stimming, silence, honesty, softness, sensory needs
- Don't punish or correct traits like lack of eye contact, bluntness, or fidgeting—these are not flaws
- Offer alternatives to high-pressure socializing—allow texting instead of calling, or parallel play-style connections
- Make space for realness—create environments where vulnerability isn't penalized or pathologized
- Affirm authenticity—validate when someone shows up in their unmasked state, especially if it's awkward, emotional, or different
- Allow opt-outs and pauses—especially in social, academic, or workplace environments
- Actively invite clarity—check in without pressure, and don't assume understanding
- Avoid comments like "You seem so normal!" or "You hide it so well!" as these can be deeply invalidating
- Unmask yourself, if safe—modeling authenticity helps others feel safe doing the same

Radical Acceptance:

I'm still learning how to notice when I'm masking. Sometimes I catch it mid-sentence; other times, not until long after. But even that awareness is progress.

I no longer see masking as something to eradicate — it's something to understand. It served a purpose. It kept me safe. But now, I want more than safety. I want to be known.

Some days, I still wear the mask because it's easier. But I'm also building relationships and spaces where I don't have to. And when I catch myself performing, I try not to judge it — I just notice it, breathe, and remember that even my masked self is still me.

Some of the most surprising parts of unmasking have shown up in how I communicate. My unmasked self can come across as blunt, even rude. I skip the niceties — the hellos, the goodbyes, the small talk that's supposed to hold conversations together. My sentences are straightforward, sometimes too direct. It's not that I mean to sound harsh; it's just that when the mask is off, my words come out clear and literal, without the filters of social polish.

At home, it's taken practice — and a lot of conversations — to be able to name when that's what's happening. I've learned to say things like, *"I'm not upset; this is just my unmasked tone right now."* It helps my wife and family understand that what sounds like irritation is often just my natural way of speaking when I'm not trying to translate myself for the world.

That's part of what makes unmasking so complex: it's not all freedom and relief. Sometimes authenticity looks or sounds uncomfortable — not just for others, but for me too. It's an adjustment for everyone.

Still, I'm learning to meet myself — all versions of me — with compassion. The masked, the unmasked, the uncertain in-between. Each one did what it needed to survive, and all of them are me.

Monotropism/Hyperfocus

Definition:

Monotropism and hyperfocus are two related but distinct concepts often used to describe the way some neurodivergent brains—especially autistic and/or ADHD brains—engage with attention, focus, and interest.

Monotropism:

- Monotropism is a theory of attention, most often associated with autism.
- It describes a tendency to focus intensely on a single interest or task, often to the exclusion of everything else.
- In a monotropic brain, attention is narrow but deep—like a tunnel. It's difficult to switch between tasks or divide attention between multiple streams.
- Transitions between activities or topics can feel jarring because the brain resists shifting away from its current focus.
- Monotropism is a trait and a consistent way of experiencing the world.

Hyperfocus:

- Hyperfocus is a state of intense concentration that can occur in people with ADHD, autism, or both.

- It often arises when a task is highly stimulating, interesting, novel, or urgent.
- During hyperfocus, a person may become so absorbed that they lose track of time, bodily needs, or external surroundings.
- It is not always voluntary and can feel either productive or disruptive, depending on context.
- Hyperfocus is a state, not a trait, so it comes and goes.

For people who are both autistic and have ADHD, these two phenomena can blend together:

- Monotropism may set the stage for hyperfocus by creating a brain that already prefers deep, singular focus.
- Hyperfocus may feel like a supercharged version of monotropism—when that one channel becomes highly rewarding or urgent.
- Both experiences involve difficulty with shifting attention, which can impact everything from task-switching to emotional regulation.

What It Feels Like:

Monotropism and hyperfocus both shape the inner experience of attention in ways that can be powerful, consuming, and at times, disorienting.

They often feel like being pulled into a tunnel, where the rest of the world dims, fades, or disappears. Whether it's a special interest, a creative project, a research spiral, or even just trying to finish a task, it's not just that we *want* to focus… it's that we *have to*. There's an urgency, a gravitational pull that makes it hard—sometimes impossible—to shift away.

Time stops existing. Hunger, fatigue, or bodily discomfort fade into the background. The mind locks in, and the deeper the focus goes, the harder it becomes to resurface. This can be exhilarating when the thing we're focused on is exciting, creative, or fulfilling, but it can also be exhausting when the task is tedious or emotionally draining. Sometimes we hyperfocus out of interest. Other times, it's because we *can't stop* until it's "done" or "right."

We don't get to decide when the tunnel opens, or when it closes. One of the most unbearable parts of monotropism or hyperfocus is what happens when we're *pulled out* of it—especially suddenly. It can be something as small as someone saying "hi," asking a question, or entering the room, but the body's reaction is *massive*—your entire system internally screams.

It's not just frustration or annoyance—it's a full-body jolt, like you've been ripped away from a lifeline, like your brain was unplugged mid-thought and now it's crashing. It can feel like panic, white-hot fury, terror, or static—*but it's none of those exactly*. It's all of them, and it's *too much*.

It can look like snappiness or withdrawal, but what's actually happening is a sudden rupture in focus that leaves your nervous system scrambling to recalibrate. The tunnel collapses, and it's not just the task that's lost, it's your place in reality.

Then comes the shame, because the world doesn't understand our response. We're often left trying to apologize for a tone or reaction not about the *person* who interrupted us, but the neurological violence of being pulled too fast from a state we didn't enter lightly.

Another difficult aspect is that focus isn't always available when we need it. We might long for it when a deadline is looming, or the house needs cleaning—but the tunnel won't open. On other days, we focus so deeply we can't stop, even when we want to.

This rhythm of being all-in or completely unable to engage can create shame and confusion, especially when the world expects consistent, evenly distributed productivity. It's not that we're avoidant, lazy, or obsessed. It's that our brains are wired to *focus deeply*, and struggle with anything that requires frequent or fluid shifting.

Special Note for Parents, Partners & Caregivers

"Clean up as you go" might not be neurologically accessible.

Thanks to the combination of hyperfocus and monotropism, when I'm engaged in something—cooking, creating, or even just getting ready—my focus locks so tightly that I can only do the actual task. Everything else disappears from my brain *and* from my vision. My brain literally doesn't register anything beyond what I'm doing.

That means every single thing I touch to complete the task gets left exactly where I touched it. I don't have access to the thought that I should put something away, throw out the trash I just created, or tidy as I go. It's not that I notice and choose to ignore it—it's that the *possibility* of noticing doesn't exist in that moment.

Linda once gently asked if I ever look around and see the multiple trails of destruction I've left in my wake. The answer is no—not at all. Not until much later, after the focus has dimmed and I've re-entered broader awareness. And by that point, my executive function is usually spent. After a flurry of activity, I need to rest before cleaning up, and that rest can last anywhere from a few hours to the next day.

It's not because I don't care—it's because the cognitive resources required to both hyperfocus *and* manage peripheral awareness simply don't coexist.

If you love someone who struggles in this way, know it's not personal. We're not deliberately leaving messes behind for you to clean up. Our brains just don't flag it in the moment. Shared planning, nonjudgmental reminders, and gentle support go much further than shame. When you understand it as a neurological blind spot—not a character flaw—everything softens.

What Doesn't Help:

Interruptions. Even small or well-meaning ones. When someone is deep in a monotropic state or hyperfocus, pulling them out can feel like yanking them from their own bloodstream. It's not just annoying, it's distressing. Saying hi, or asking a simple question might seem harmless, but it feels like our entire mental scaffolding just collapsed. Rebuilding it can take hours—if it happens at all.

What also doesn't help is the belief that we should be able to *snap out of it*. Or that being "focused" is a compliment when it comes at the expense of basic needs, relationships, or regulation. Hyperfocus can be an incredible strength, but it can also be a trap. When people praise the output without understanding the cost, it reinforces the idea that we're only valuable when we're producing or achieving.

Time-blindness and monotropism often team up—and it doesn't help when others assume we're being rude, flaky, or avoidant because we didn't respond to a message, forgot to eat, or missed a plan. We weren't ignoring you; we were lost inside a tunnel with no exits. The guilt of this misinterpretation can be enormous, especially when we resurface and realize the damage.

Then there's the shame of being pulled out of a hyperfocus and realizing you forgot something important. The shame of neglecting your body, your people, or your life. The shame of not being able to recreate the same focus the next day, even though you *really* need to. That shame doesn't motivate, it paralyzes. What doesn't help is when people minimize that experience, or say things like "take a break," "eat something," or "set a timer." If only it were that easy.

Most systems aren't built for these kinds of brains. School, work, family schedules—they're often structured around multitasking, fast transitions, and divided attention. But monotropism doesn't play well with divided attention. When we're forced to stretch ourselves too thinly, constantly shifting from one thing to the next, we don't just struggle—we unravel.

What does help:

Protecting the tunnel. Not forever, or at the expense of everything else, but with intention. If I know I'm going into hyperfocus, or monotropism is pulling me in, I try to set up a supportive space around me. I fill a water bottle, set a snack nearby, let my wife know I may be off-grid for a while. When I do that, I'm not abandoning the world—I'm setting boundaries that honor how my brain works best.

It also helps to be interrupted gently, if at all. If someone *must* interrupt, a light touch on the arm, a soft voice, or even texting me first gives my nervous system a bit of a landing strip. No loud entrances. No sudden questions. No "Hey, real quick..." because there's no such thing as "real quick" when I'm deep in something. Every shift is a detour, so gentle rerouting gives me the best chance of returning afterward.

What really helps, though, is letting go of guilt. If I hyperfocus on something and forget to eat, I don't spend the rest of the day shaming myself, I just eat. If I miss a text or don't come out of the tunnel in time for something, I acknowledge it, repair the situation, and remind myself that I wasn't checked out—I was tuned in. That's not a failure, it's just how I'm wired.

The biggest thing that helps is being understood. When people around me know that this is part of how I function—not a flaw, a choice, or a personal slight—it changes everything. I don't have to over-explain. I don't have to apologize for being myself. I can be in the tunnel *and* still feel connected. That's the difference between hyperfocus as a superpower and hyperfocus as a survival strategy.

Accommodations:

- Protect hyperfocus time when possible. If a person is deeply engaged in something meaningful or productive, try not to interrupt unless absolutely necessary. Let them finish the loop.
- Use gentle, non-disruptive cues to signal breaks. Light touches, soft tones, or pre-agreed signals (like a timer or a note) can help someone withdraw from hyperfocus without triggering a full-body startle.

- Time-anchor with external tools. Visual timers, hourly chimes, soft alarms, or ambient soundtracks can help mark time without breaking focus completely.
- Pre-load basic needs. Before diving into a focus tunnel, set up snacks, water, bathroom breaks, or anything else that might prevent total depletion.
- Schedule buffer time after hyperfocus. Coming out of it can feel jarring, so allow space to rest, transition, or recalibrate before expecting more interaction or output.
- Provide reminders with kindness and context. Instead of "You forgot again," try "Hey, I know it's hard to shift out of deep focus. Do you need help wrapping this up?"
- Avoid shaming after the fact. If someone forgets something while hyperfocused (eating, texting back, showing up), skip the guilt trip. Offer support, not scolding.
- Encourage low-stakes reentry after hyperfocus. Coming out of a deep-focus state can be *exhausting*. Even if it looked like we were "just sitting there," our brains were running a full marathon. It helps to re-enter gently with grounding, no-pressure tasks like stretching, drinking water, stepping outside, or doing something familiar and soothing. Don't expect us to jump right into the next thing. Let our nervous system catch up.
- Honor the importance of the interest. Even if it seems niche or unimportant to others, monotropism means the topic holds emotional and cognitive weight. Respect that.
- Educate loved ones and coworkers. Helping others understand what hyperfocus or monotropism looks like —and why it's not a sign of being aloof or obsessive— can reduce tension and increase support.

Radical Acceptance:

Radical acceptance starts with letting go of the guilt. Letting go of the idea that we should be able to evenly spread our focus, or flip effortlessly between topics, or always answer a text in the middle of writing something. Personally, I can't. My attention runs deep, not wide.

Hyperfocus can be incredibly productive, but it can also be a trap. I can lose time, forget to eat, ignore my body's signals, or go past the point of fatigue. And when I'm finally out of hyperfocus, I often feel disoriented, flooded, and shattered. It's a strange mix of brilliance and burnout. But rather than trying to "fix" it, I've learned to *honor* it.

I've stopped fighting the tides of my focus and started learning to surf them. I build my life around what works for me: protecting long stretches of uninterrupted time, creating gentle on-ramps and off-ramps around my work, and giving myself time to recover after an intense focus session. I no longer expect myself to be "always available."

Radical acceptance also means helping the people around me understand my neurological processes, so they don't take it personally when I don't respond right away or seem "locked in." It helps them know not to interrupt unless necessary—and if they do, to approach with care. It also means giving myself patience and compassion when I inevitably crash, because emerging from hyperfocus is its own kind of comedown, and I deserve care in that space too. When someone *does* interrupt and I respond more sharply than I mean to, I can name what's happening with honesty—and that can shift the entire dynamic.

This isn't about glorifying tunnel vision or pretending it doesn't have a cost. It's about respecting the truth of how my brain works and building a rhythm around it that allows me to thrive. I may never be a multitasker or an easy shifter. But I can be a deep diver, a passionate creator, and a person who gives their full self to what they love.

Neurodivergent System Overload – Overwhelm, Meltdowns, Shutdowns, and Burnout

Definition: Neurodivergent System Overload is what happens when a person's sensory, emotional, cognitive, or social input exceeds what their system can manage. While everyone experiences stress and overstimulation at times, neurodivergent people (especially those with ADHD, Autism, and PDA profiles) often have more sensitive or differently wired nervous systems, making overload more frequent, more intense, and harder to recover from.

System overload isn't a single event—it's a spectrum. Understanding the four primary ways it shows up can help you recognize, respond to, and even prevent some of the most misunderstood aspects of the neurodivergent experience.

The Four Expressions of Neurodivergent Overload:

- Overwhelm – The buildup. A state of input overload where everything starts to feel "too much." This is often the first warning sign.

- Meltdown – The eruption. A visible, often explosive release of built-up stress or distress. Meltdowns are not tantrums, they are nervous system floods.
- Shutdown – The retreat. A quiet but intense internal collapse where the person may go nonverbal, dissociate, or simply stop functioning.
- Burnout – The crash. A long-term state of physical, emotional, and cognitive depletion caused by chronic masking, overextension, and unresolved overload.

These are not character flaws. They are adaptive responses from a nervous system trying to survive in a world that often demands too much, too fast, too loudly.

Neurodivergent Overwhelm

Definition:
Overwhelm is the first wave of neurodivergent system overload. It happens when sensory, emotional, cognitive, or social inputs stack up faster than the brain can process. It can feel like everything is too much, too loud, too bright, too fast, too demanding, too emotional. Many neurodivergent people operate with heightened sensitivity or have less buffer in their nervous system, so it doesn't take a major crisis to tip the scales. Sometimes, all it takes is a small interruption, a change in plans, a loud noise, or too many open tabs in the brain.

Overwhelm isn't a meltdown, but it's often the red flag stage—the body is sounding the alarm for low capacity. For some, overwhelm feels like panic or chaos. For others, it's more like a fog setting in—slower thinking, irritability, forgetfulness, the inability to prioritize. It can also cause physical symptoms like headaches, nausea, or fatigue.

What it feels like:
I was constantly living in a state of overwhelm until I finally had the language to name it. For most of my life, I just thought I was bad at handling things—too sensitive and emotional, too disorganized, too reactive. Now I know I was constantly flooded with more input than my system could handle, but instead of seeing that as a warning sign, I tried to push through. I thought the solution was to be stronger, to focus harder, to keep trying all the tools in the self-help toolkit—meditation, gratitude, breathing exercises—anything to convince myself it wasn't happening.

What's wild is that when you've lived in overwhelm your whole life without realizing, you can mask so hard you don't even know you're overwhelmed. I didn't know how much noise affected me until I tried noise-canceling earplugs, and suddenly, I could take a full breath. There were clues, sure: I could hear things no one else noticed. I never liked loud music, hated going to the movies (not just for the volume, but the cold and brightness), and over time, I developed a real aversion to the TV. But if you'd asked me, I wouldn't have said I was sensitive to sound. And lights practically attack my nervous system too. Long before I had words for any of this, I had already unscrewed all but one bulb in every overhead lights, and I'd drape a scarf over it just to soften the brightness (despite my wife's concern that it was a fire hazard, which it totally was). I didn't know these things were contributing to overwhelm; I just thought they were odd quirks.

Overwhelm shows up as noise in my brain—like a hundred radios playing at once, each on different stations. It's not just mental clutter, it's full-body chaos. Everything becomes too loud, too fast, too much. The texture of my clothes, the sound of someone chewing, an overhead light—it all piles on. My thoughts blur together like static, my emotions surge without warning, and I can't sort out what's urgent or what makes sense. I stare blankly, paralyzed by the sheer volume of input. I become irrationally panicked over the hum of a fan or the ticking of a clock, sounds that most people are not even registering. I snap at someone I love, not because I'm angry, but because I can't process one more question, one more demand, one more anything—even if it's kind or simple.

In those moments, the world doesn't feel safe or manageable. It feels unpredictable, unsafe, and unkind. And that's really what overwhelm *is*: a full-system safety response. My nervous system interprets the overflow as danger and begins to shift into survival mode. To others, it might look like a mood swing, a bad attitude, or rudeness. But what's really happening is system overload—my internal wiring sparking and shutting down under too much pressure. It is completely overwhelming. No amount of logic or willpower can bring me back to baseline until I find safety, quiet, and time.

What's especially tricky is how easy it is to misread overwhelm. It can look and feel like anxiety. It can look and feel like mood swings. It can look and feel like someone being dramatic, sensitive, flaky, or "too much." Sometimes it doesn't look or feel like anything at all—it just shows up as quiet withdrawal, flat affect, or odd little habits that no one thinks twice about. I spent years trying to manage what I thought were separate problems: anxiety, irritability, reactivity, indecision, exhaustion. But they were all coming from overwhelm. I didn't recognize that, and neither did anyone else.

What doesn't help:

When overwhelm strikes, attempts to explain, rationalize, or encourage logical thinking often add to the cognitive load. The overwhelmed brain can't cope with processing more input (even if it is kind or helpful). It can make things much worse.

Phrases like "calm down," "just breathe," or "you're overreacting" tend to invalidate the experience and increase shame. Even well-meaning reassurances can feel dismissive when someone is in sensory or emotional overload. What's needed is not instruction, but relief.

Asking questions or demanding decisions during a period of overwhelm can increase distress. The ability to prioritize, process, and respond is often compromised, and pressure to perform or engage can push someone further toward shutdown, meltdown, or dissociation.

Expecting someone to push through, stay on task, or continue engaging socially can be deeply dysregulating. Overwhelm is not about willpower or attitude—it's a nervous system response. Misinterpreting it as laziness, disrespect, or over-sensitivity only deepens disconnection and can cause long-term harm to self-trust and relationships.

What does help:

Regulation, not reasoning, is the key to helping overwhelm. Overwhelm isn't a choice or a mindset—it's the nervous system signaling *unsafety* and the need for protection. The most effective support often starts with reducing input and offering safety. That might look like dimming the lights, lowering noise, pausing a conversation, or stepping into a quieter space.

Permission to pause is key—being allowed to step away, take a break, or disengage without guilt or pressure creates the conditions for recovery. Validation is also powerful. Simple phrases like "It's okay to feel overwhelmed" or "Let's slow things down" can help signal safety to the brain. A calm, steady presence often does more than any solution or advice ever could.

For people who often experience overwhelm, proactive planning can also make a big difference—things like minimizing transitions, reducing decision-making, and scheduling recovery time after high-demand situations.

Responses rooted in understanding and gentleness can help build a sense of internal safety, turning moments of overload into manageable experiences.

Accommodations:

- Reduce sensory input when possible — dim lighting, lower volume, offer noise-canceling headphones or sunglasses, minimize environmental clutter
- Create quiet retreat spaces — a designated calm zone at home, school, or work where the person can go to regulate without being questioned or interrupted.
- Offer flexible transitions — provide advance notice for changes, avoid abrupt switches between tasks or environments.
- Use visual supports — visual schedules, step-by-step guides, or written instructions can reduce cognitive load.
- Minimize verbal demands during overwhelm — avoid asking questions, giving instructions, or initiating conversations when someone is dysregulated.

- Allow for nonverbal communication — gestures, hand signals, or visual cards to express needs like "I need a break" or "Too much right now."
- Normalize breaks — integrate rest or sensory breaks into daily routines, not just in crisis moments.
- Pre-schedule recovery time — after high-demand situations (social events, appointments, etc.), build in buffer periods with no expectations.
- Limit decision fatigue — offer choices in manageable formats (e.g., "Would you like A or B?"), or pre-plan meals, outfits, or routines.
- Honor self-regulation strategies — allow stimming, movement, fidgets, pacing, or any soothing activity unless it's harmful.
- Avoid public correction or redirection — when support is needed, offer it privately and gently to prevent additional shame or shutdown.
- Use routines and predictability — familiar structure reduces cognitive load and emotional uncertainty.
- Be an emotional anchor — remain calm and grounded, using steady body language and tone to signal safety.
- Offer co-regulation if welcomed — sitting quietly together, breathing in sync, or engaging in a low-demand shared activity can help.

Radical Acceptance:

Radical acceptance of my overwhelm didn't come easily. For most of my life, I treated it like something to fix or hide. I kept trying to become the kind of person who could handle more noise, pressure, and expectations. But no matter how hard I pushed myself, my system kept breaking. I thought that meant I was broken.

But now, I know better.

I know that my nervous system has limits—and honoring those limits is not a weakness, it's wisdom. I no longer try to force myself through overwhelm with grit and shame. I don't measure my worth by how much I can tolerate. I measure it by how well I listen to my body, how quickly I notice the signs, and how gently I respond.

Radical acceptance means I take myself seriously before I collapse. It means I don't apologize for needing quiet, space, or softness. It means I give myself permission to step away and care for myself the way I wish someone had cared for me.

Overwhelm is not a flaw in my design. It's a signal. When I treat it like one—when I slow down, listen, and respond with compassion—I don't just survive, I rebuild self-trust. I become safer inside my own body. That's the work I'm finally learning how to do.

Neurodivergent Meltdowns

Definition:

A neurodivergent meltdown is an intense, involuntary nervous system response to overwhelming stress, often triggered when cognitive, emotional, sensory, or social demands exceed a person's capacity to cope.

Unlike tantrums, meltdowns are not intentional or manipulative. They are a form of neurological flooding where the brain's regulatory systems are overwhelmed, and the ability to self-modulate breaks down. During a meltdown, an overwhelmed person may experience uncontrollable crying, yelling, pacing, hitting, throwing objects, or self-injurious behaviors. Meltdowns can also manifest more internally, such as intense irritability, rage, crying spells, or shutting down physically or verbally.

Meltdowns are not a failure of emotional control but a protective mechanism of the nervous system under extreme distress. They often occur after prolonged masking, accumulated micro-stressors, transitions, sensory overload, invalidation, or high social or emotional pressure.

Post-meltdown exhaustion is common and may last hours or days. Providing a safe, nonjudgmental environment before, during, and after a meltdown is critical for recovery and long-term regulation.

What It Feels Like:

A meltdown doesn't feel like an overreaction, even though it can look like it—it feels like a detonation. It's not a choice, not a moment of bad behavior or poor attitude. It's what happens when my system has taken in more than it can hold, and every thread finally snaps. Sometimes it comes on fast—a sound or disruption, confrontation, or something breaking my routine—and I'm suddenly flooded. Other times, it builds quietly in the background for days, even weeks, until one small thing tips me over the edge.

In those moments, my body becomes hijacked. I might yell, cry, clench my fists, shake, slam a door and often say things I don't mean. The feeling is visceral, like I'm drowning in a wave of heat, sound, emotion, and pressure, and my only options are to scream or collapse. I can't think logically or respond calmly. I'm not in control of my words or tone. My nervous system is in full-blown survival mode.

Sometimes I disassociate mid-meltdown, like I'm watching myself from elsewhere. Afterward, I'm emotionally and physically wrecked, and in the past, I'd also be cloaked in shame. Most people see only the eruption; they don't see the mountain of effort it takes to internalize everything for so long. The meltdown is never just about what happened in that moment—it's the cumulative weight of too many things.

It's hard to describe how deeply *out of control* it feels, and how much internal pain is wrapped inside that loss of control. But I've also learned something vital: meltdowns are part of my neurodivergent experience. They aren't personal failures, and I can reduce their frequency. I can better support myself, but I can't stop them. Pretending they don't happen—or blaming myself when they do—only adds to the shame. Meltdowns are not me being bad. They're what happens when I've carried too much, for too long, with too little support.

What doesn't help:

When a neurodivergent person is experiencing a meltdown, additional pressure, expectation, or invalidation is damaging. Telling us to calm down, asking us to explain ourselves, or trying to get us to "use our tools" usually backfires. It might seem helpful from the outside, but our rational, thinking brain has gone offline—there's no access to logic, language, or emotional control. Even gentle questions like "What do you need?" or "What's wrong?" can feel like being handed a pop quiz during a house fire. Punishment, scolding, or shaming— including the subtler versions like disappointed sighs or "Come on, you're fine"—tend to deepen the meltdown or lock in long-lasting shame. Touch can be soothing for some and unbearable for others, but either way, uninvited contact in that moment often feels invasive.

Trying to reason with us or explain why we're overreacting only increases the overwhelm. It's also deeply unhelpful when people judge what triggered the meltdown. It might seem small to them, but it's never just about the thing that tipped us over. It's about the buildup and the pressure, the sensory load and social confusion, the bottled-up stress, the skipped meals, and the ignored boundaries. When someone meets our meltdown with their own big emotions, especially anger or panic, it often makes us feel unsafe and even more dysregulated. Meltdowns are not a choice, a tantrum, or a character flaw. They're the result of a system hitting its limit. We can absolutely learn tools to reduce their impact over time, but in the moment, what we need most is space, calm, and safety.

What does help:

What helps during a neurodivergent meltdown is not fixing, explaining, or reasoning—it's co-regulation, gentleness, and nervous system safety. The most supportive thing anyone can do is stay grounded and create a calm, low-demand environment. Often, the best approach is quiet presence—no words or questions, just a calm energy that signals "you're not in trouble, and you're not alone." Soft lighting, reduced noise, limited movement—these all help minimize sensory input. Giving space is also important, but space doesn't have to mean abandonment. It can mean sitting nearby without expectations or stepping away briefly while letting the person know you're still available. If the person has previously identified what helps them regulate, offering access to those tools (without forcing them) can be helpful. For some, deep pressure or a long, steady hug might be exactly what they need, but only if it's something they've asked for or have indicated is okay. After the meltdown has passed, compassion without analysis is key: no lecture, no "what could you have done differently," just a soft landing and maybe a snack. Later, when the system is back online, there may be room for reflection, pattern recognition, or accommodations, but none of that is helpful until the storm has cleared. Ultimately, it helps to be seen not as a problem to solve, but as a nervous system in distress—one that needs care, not correction.

Accommodations:

- Low-demand periods during the day (scheduled sensory or decompression breaks)
- Access to a quiet space to regulate when overwhelmed (sensory room, car, designated room)
- Noise-canceling headphones or earplugs to reduce auditory overload
- Visual schedules or reminders to reduce surprise and transition stress
- Reduced verbal instruction, especially during high-stress moments—offer written or visual support instead
- Flexible deadlines or modified workloads to prevent pressure overload
- Permission to leave or pause during overwhelming situations without needing to explain
- Fidgets, chewies, or stimming tools to self-regulate without shame
- Predictable routines and advance notice of changes whenever possible
- Safe words or signals to indicate a need for help or a break without needing to verbalize

- Supportive nearby adult or peer who understands how to co-regulate and won't escalate the situation
- Option for alternative environments (e.g., learning or working from home, reduced hours, outdoor workspaces)
- Avoiding high-stakes situations that rely on verbal processing under pressure (oral presentations, public confrontation)
- Access to sensory supports like weighted blankets, compression vests, dim lighting, or calming visuals
- No punitive responses to meltdowns—understanding they are neurological, not behavioral
- Allowing movement breaks or body-based regulation (walking, swinging, stretching)
- Clear communication of expectations and boundaries, delivered calmly and consistently
- Validation and empathy after a meltdown, without immediate conversation or repair

Radical Acceptance:

It took me a long time to stop seeing meltdowns as personal failures by me and my daughter. I felt shame. Every time, I felt like I should've seen it coming or done something differently to prevent it. Afterward, I would spiral, trying to dissect every detail, searching for the one thing I missed. But the truth is, meltdowns are part of being neurodivergent. The more I understood the full-body nature of neurodivergence—how sensory load, social energy, emotional suppression, and executive dysfunction all pile up—the more I could soften my lens. Now, when a meltdown happens, I don't fight it. I don't rush to fix it. I try to get grounded and stay close, either to myself or to the person experiencing the meltdown. I remind myself that it isn't a disaster, it's a passing storm. The nervous system will come back online, not because I forced it, but because I made space.

Radical acceptance doesn't mean giving up on growth or support, it means releasing the illusion that we can love or logic our way out of being differently wired. It means making peace with our thresholds and building lives that honor them. I no longer ask, "How do I make sure this never happens again?" I ask, "How can I reduce the frequency?" "How do I create softness around the experience?" and "How do I comfort myself afterwards?"

Neurodivergent Shutdown

Definition: Shutdown is a neurodivergent response to overwhelm, often triggered when the nervous system is pushed beyond its capacity to cope emotionally, cognitively, or physically. Unlike meltdowns, which tend to be outward and explosive, a shutdown is inward and collapsing. It can look like withdrawal, silence, dissociation, freezing, or a complete inability to speak, move, or respond to others. For many neurodivergent people shutdowns are not a choice or a dramatic reaction. They are a form of protection for the brain and body to survive overload.

Shutdowns can be triggered by sensory input, emotional intensity, decision fatigue, social exhaustion, or persistent masking. They may last minutes, hours, or even days. During a shutdown, the individual often feels disconnected from their environment and unable to communicate their needs. They may appear "fine" to others, while internally, they are struggling to function.

What It feels like:

For me, shutdowns come in two distinct and disorienting forms. Most commonly, everything goes dark. My brain shuts down alongside my body, and I can't form coherent thoughts or words. I can't move. It's like a black hole opens up in my mind, and I'm unreachable—even to myself. Other times, my body shuts down, but my brain ramps up like I'm trapped on a chaotic fairground ride. My thoughts spin wildly while my body freezes. No one would guess from looking at me that an internal storm is raging. Both versions leave me feeling powerless, distant, alone, and often misunderstood.

Accommodations:

- Allow for quiet, low-demand environments when possible. Overstimulation or emotional overwhelm require time and space to recover from. This might mean a dark room, noise-canceling headphones, or permission to step away.
- Offer support without pressure. Gentle presence can be more regulating than questions or problem-solving. A simple "I'm here if you need me" goes a long way.
- Use nonverbal check-ins when verbal processing isn't possible. Texting instead of talking is a low-pressure way of communicating, or try offering a comforting item like a blanket or snack.
- Build in recovery time after high-stress situations. Shutdown often follows cumulative stress, so giving space after big events or social interaction is protective.
- Help identify shutdown triggers ahead of time. Sensory overload, too many decisions, and emotional conflict are draining, so it's vital to plan or pivot when needed.

- Reduce expectations during a shutdown. Don't ask the person to make decisions, respond immediately, or explain what's happening. Their system may be offline.
- Support gentle transitions back into engagement. A soft routine, warm drink, familiar music, or favorite show can help someone reenter the world without additional demands.
- Schedule downtime or shutdown periods. If you are prone to shutdowns and can't yet avoid them, a preemptive shutdown is far easier to manage than one that arrives unannounced.

Radical Acceptance:

For me, radical acceptance of shutdowns meant finally understanding that they aren't laziness, weakness, or failure. My body and brain are not giving up; they're shutting down to protect me from complete collapse. Once I stopped trying to power through or snap myself out of it, things got better. I started to build my life around prevention and recovery instead of shame and self-punishment.

Linda now knows that when I become quiet and disappear for a while, it's not rejection, it's regulation. I've gotten better at spotting the early signs of shutdown, but often, Linda notices them before I do. In those moments, I give myself permission to pause—or Linda gently but firmly encourages me to. When I do shut down, I treat myself like someone who needs care, instead of someone who failed. It's a shift that has changed everything. It's helped me meet myself with kindness, and it's made the shutdowns less frightening and isolating, and often, a little shorter. They're still hard, but they're no longer laced with shame or confusion.

Neurodivergent Burnout

Definition: This is a profound and often debilitating state of physical, mental, and emotional exhaustion that occurs when the ongoing demands of navigating a neurotypical world exceed a neurodivergent person's capacity to cope. It is not the same as general burnout—it is more intense, longer-lasting, and rooted in chronic masking, sensory overload, social exhaustion, executive dysfunction, and unmet access needs.

Unlike typical burnout, neurodivergent burnout often includes a loss of previously accessible skills (such as speaking, functioning at work, or completing basic self-care tasks), increased sensory sensitivity, heightened emotional reactivity or shutdown, and an overwhelming sense of detachment or despair.

What it feels like:

Neurodivergent burnout feels like the moment your body and brain slam on the brakes, but you've already gone off the cliff. I couldn't function, think, or recover only through rest. It wasn't "being tired." It was an emptying—physically, emotionally, and mentally. The worst part was that I didn't know what was happening. If I had known then what I know now—that this level of collapse is a known neurodivergent experience—I might have been more self-compassionate, and most likely would have caught it sooner.

Accommodations:

- Redesign your life—not just your schedule. Rest alone won't fix burnout if the life you're returning to is

unsustainable. Major structural changes may be necessary.
- Identify and eliminate chronic stressors—including sensory overwhelm, toxic environments, unrealistic expectations, or social overload.
- Say no more often—to things that don't seem possible to avoid, and don't apologize for it. Boundaries are survival, not selfishness.
- Prioritize recovery time—daily, weekly, and seasonally. Build in real rest and decompression time as a permanent fixture, not a reward.
- Simplify everything—routines, meals, responsibilities, relationships. Complexity fuels burnout.
- Lower the bar—aim for sustainable, not superhuman. "Good enough" is often more than enough.
- Build a life that matches your capacity—not your ideals, not others' expectations, and not who you wish you could be on a perfect day.
- Avoid going back to burnout-inducing systems—even if they paid the bills, made you look successful, or once felt important.
- Find or create environments where you can unmask—whether that's at home, online, in therapy, or among trusted people.
- Schedule shutdowns or low-demand days if you're prone to unplanned collapses— it's much easier to navigate when it's expected and supported.
- Track your energy, not just your time—and adjust accordingly. Energy is the true currency of sustainable living.

Radical Acceptance:

Radical acceptance of neurodivergent burnout means understanding that it wasn't a personal failure, it was a system failure. A mismatch between my wiring and the demands of the world I was trying to survive in. I now see burnout as a serious warning sign that my life needs to change. It's not a fluke or weakness, it's a predictable outcome when I override my needs for too long. Radical acceptance means honoring my limits, even when they're inconvenient or misunderstood. It means letting go of who I thought I *should* be and building a life that supports who I *am*. I no longer wait to "earn" rest, or shame myself for needing recovery time. I listen earlier, pause more often, and treat myself with care.

As a parent, radical acceptance means letting go of the fantasy that my child's educational path will look like everyone else's—or even what I imagined it would be. It means recognizing that Keleigh's school burnout wasn't laziness, defiance, or lack of ability—it was a full-body response to chronic overwhelm, unmet needs, and constant misattunement. Accepting this doesn't mean giving up on Keleigh's learning, it means redefining what that learning can look like. It's choosing relationship and regulation over rigid expectations. It's meeting her where she is and building a life with her, not around her. When I stopped trying to force her to fit into systems that were harming her, everything softened. She started to come back to life.

Closing Thoughts: Living with (and within) our limits:

Overwhelm, meltdowns, shutdowns, burnout—these are not isolated events. They're not failures of character or lapses in willpower. They are the body's way of saying, "This is too much." They are what happens when the world demands more than our systems can safely give. They are a part of our experience. While they're deeply misunderstood by many, they're a core part of our neurodivergent experience.

Learning to recognize these patterns early and without shame has changed everything. I no longer see my limits as weaknesses to overcome, but as boundaries to be respected. I've learned that safety, softness, and sustainability are not luxuries. They are the ground I need in order to show up at all.

This work isn't just about personal recovery, it's about cultural reclamation. It's about building lives, relationships, schools, workplaces, and communities that don't push people to the edge just to be seen as valuable. It's about changing the question from "How can we make you fit?" to "What would this look like if it actually worked for you?"

And most of all, it's about choosing compassion over compliance, again and again.

Whether you're someone living with these experiences yourself, or are someone loving a neurodivergent person, know this: we are not broken. We are not too much. We are not a problem to be solved. We are people trying to live in a world that often doesn't understand our wiring. But we're learning how to understand ourselves. We're learning how to listen. How to soften. How to stay.

And in that process we're not just surviving, we're becoming whole.

Object and People Impermanence

Definition: Object and people impermanence refer to the tendency to lose awareness of things or people when they are not immediately present.

Object impermanence means that if an item is out of sight, it may effectively disappear from working memory, making it difficult to recall or act on. This can affect tasks like remembering food in the fridge, ongoing projects, or stored belongings.

People impermanence is difficulty maintaining emotional connection or mental awareness of others when they are not physically present or actively engaging. This can result in unintentionally losing touch or feeling distant from loved ones, despite caring deeply about them.

These challenges are rooted in differences in working memory, attention regulation, and the way neurodivergent brains process presence and time.

What It Feels Like:

Living with a neurodivergent brain—especially an AuDHD one—often means existing inside a web of paradoxes. I can't hold on to the name of someone I just met, but I can tell you exactly where a specific safety pin with a sticker on it lives, even though I haven't seen it in 20 years. I forget that people I love exist when they're not in my immediate visual field, but I can remember the lyrics to a song I heard once as a child. I lose track of the conversation I'm in, but I can mentally catalog the layout of a junk drawer from a house I haven't lived in for a decade.

That's the maddening, inexplicable paradox of object and people impermanence. I constantly forget everything. I walk into another room, and everyone I care about disappears from my mental map. Not emotionally—they still matter—but they don't feel *present*. It's like my brain is a flashlight, and whatever's not in the beam is simply… gone. Out of sight, out of mind, in the most literal, disorienting way.

This isn't detachment, and it's not that I don't care. It's that my brain can't hold onto things that aren't currently being lit up by my attention—and sometimes that includes the people I love most. I forget to text back, forget birthdays, forget whole humans—until they're in front of me again and my heart floods with recognition and guilt. It feels pretty crummy..

How do you tell someone: *"I didn't mean to ignore you—I just literally forgot you existed for a little while."* That kind of honesty feels brutal, but it's the truth. None of this means I care any less. It just means my brain holds presence differently.

Sometimes when Keleigh is at a friend's house or off doing something, Linda will ask me if I've heard from her or when she's getting home, and it'll hit me like a lightning bolt: *Oh my God. I completely forgot about her.*

It always feels horrifying to say that out loud, because you know I fought like hell for that child. I love her more than I can possibly express. And yet, if she's not physically in my awareness, my brain just drops the thread. It doesn't matter how deeply I love her and that she's my world, she goes off radar until something pings her back into my field.

I think that moment proves what I've come to understand: this isn't about caring. This isn't about attachment or love or priority. It's just the way my brain works. If my brain can do this with the person I love most in the world, then it *must* be neurological. Love doesn't solve it. Connection doesn't fix it. Only presence does. And that's no one's fault.

What doesn't help:

Assuming this is about love, interest, or priority. It's not that we don't care, it's that our brains can't hold onto things that aren't right in front of us. Telling us not to care, or asking us how we could forget, only adds shame to something that's already confusing and painful for us, too.

What also doesn't help is assuming that reminders will be insulting. Most of us *need* reminders—sometimes a lot of them. We need nudges, not judgments. What feels frustrating to others (like repeating something or checking in again) might be the exact thing that allows us to reconnect and re-engage.

Another thing that doesn't help is expecting consistency. Some days, I *can* hold people in mind, even when they're not here. Other days, it's like my brain is a snow globe and someone shook it—nothing sticks. The inconsistency is maddening even to me. I don't like that I can remember where to find a safety pin from 1996, but I can forget someone I deeply love exists the minute they leave the house. It's not personal, it's a paradox. Being accused of neglect or carelessness only deepens the spiral of shame.

Silence is incredibly unhelpful. When people don't understand this, they fill in the blanks themselves. And those blanks often get filled with hurt. People think we're cold, self-centered, or unreliable, but that couldn't be further from the truth. We *do* care. We *do* love. Our brains just have a unique way of holding onto things—and sometimes that means not holding them at all unless they're right in front of us.

What Does Help:

Naming the experience lessens the shame. When I say out loud, "I literally forgot Keleigh existed for a minute," it sounds wild, but it's the truth. It gives the people I love a window into what's happening inside my brain, instead of them trying to interpret my silence or apparent distance.

What also helps are systems of connection. Sticky notes, shared calendars, location-sharing apps, routines that bring people back into my awareness. Even a photo on the fridge. Anything that gives my brain a hook—something to tether that person or task to the present moment.

Check-ins help too, especially when they're framed gently. "Hey, have you thought about calling your mom today?" goes a lot further than, "I can't believe you forgot." Supportive reminders don't shame me, they anchor me and help me return.

What helps most is compassion from others and from myself. None of this is a failure of love; it's a neurological pattern. The more I understand it, the less I spiral when it happens. I can say, "Oh, this is my brain doing that thing again," instead of "What kind of monster forgets their own kid?"

When I share that with the people close to me—when I let them in on the pattern—they stop taking it personally, too. It softens things. It helps us laugh instead of argue. And it reminds all of us that this is something we can navigate together with grace, instead of shame.

Accommodations:

- Visual anchors: Keep photos, names, or written reminders of important people and tasks in visible places (walls, mirrors, fridge, digital wallpapers). Out of sight truly can mean out of mind.
- Frequent gentle check-ins: Build routines where loved ones check in by text, voice note, or presence—not as pressure, but as a grounding tether. Structure helps, spontaneity often disappears.
- Externalize everything: Use calendars, whiteboards, sticky notes, app reminders—whatever helps offload the cognitive work of "holding" people and responsibilities in your mind.
- Shared systems: Use shared digital tools (Google calendars, notes, lists, tracking apps) to keep each other visible and connected. This is especially helpful for family life or caregiving roles.
- Relationship rituals: Create regular rhythms of connection—like "family check-in at dinner" or "text-your-friend Thursdays"—to help maintain presence even when memory falters.
- Compassion scripts: Teach family and friends to use supportive language like, "Want a little reminder?" or "Can I help bring this back into your awareness?" instead of using shame or blame.
- Body and environmental cues: Use familiar scents, music, objects, or routines associated with a person to

help maintain connection or recall. Sensory anchoring helps bridge the gap.
- Normalize re-entry: Allow for a warm-up period when reconnecting—emotionally or cognitively—with people you haven't seen in a bit. A "mental reset" can go a long way.
- Say it out loud: Practice openly acknowledging impermanence when it happens ("Oh wow, I totally forgot!") to reduce shame and help others understand it's neurological, not emotional.

Radical acceptance:

Forgetting someone I love so deeply used to wreck me with shame. How could I walk into a room, see an object I cherish, and feel shocked to remember it exists? It felt like a character flaw—like I was too self-absorbed or emotionally stunted. But now I realize this isn't a lack of love or value. It's a brain thing, and the more I fight it, the more shame grows.

Radical acceptance means letting go of the idea that memory equals care, or that presence equals importance. It means understanding that just because I forget someone exists when they're not right in front of me, doesn't mean I don't love them with every cell of my body. My attention and awareness are not broad. They're deep and narrow. If someone isn't inside that narrow beam, they can vanish from my active consciousness.

None of this makes me a bad partner, parent, or friend. It makes me a person with an AuDHD brain. One that loves hard, remembers odd and beautiful details from decades ago, and sometimes forgets their own child exists for a few hours while they're out of sight.

Radical acceptance is how I unhook from guilt. It's how I explain it to Linda or Keleigh without apology, but with clarity and care. It's how I stop pretending I can "just remember better" and instead build the systems that help me stay connected in the ways my brain actually works.

Most importantly, it's how I help shift the story for the people I love so they don't internalize my forgetfulness as a measure of their worth. I say it out loud. I name it. I laugh gently when I say, "Oh my god, I totally forgot about her," not because I don't care, but because I do. It makes space for everyone to feel safer in the truth, not more hidden in the fear.

PDA – Pathological Demand Avoidance (Persistent Drive for Autonomy)

Definition: Pathological Demand Avoidance, or Persistent Drive for Autonomy, is a profile of neurodivergence characterized by an intense, subconscious, anxiety-driven need to avoid everyday demands, expectations, or perceived pressures. These demands can be external (like being asked to get dressed) or internal (like wanting to do something but feeling unable).

At its core, PDA is not about defiance or willful noncompliance—it's a nervous system-based threat response. For individuals with PDA, even simple or self-imposed demands can trigger intense autonomic arousal. The brain interprets the demand as a threat to autonomy or safety, activating the fight, flight, freeze, or fawn response. This often results in refusal, avoidance, shutdowns, meltdowns, or people-pleasing behaviors.

The avoidance itself is often strategic, creative, and subconscious, which can make it especially confusing to others. What may look like manipulation or defiance is actually an attempt to equalize a perceived threat. This nervous system dysregulation leads to high baseline anxiety, difficulty with emotional regulation, and extreme sensitivity to pressure.

PDA is frequently seen in individuals with neurodivergence, especially those with co-occurring trauma, heightened sensitivity, or a history of being misunderstood. It is not rare, but it is often missed or mischaracterized—especially in children, where it can show up as refusal to do basic tasks, aggressive or explosive behavior, or sudden shutdowns after seemingly minor requests.

The equalizing behavior is often the clue because it rarely matches the situation in a "logical" way. It might look like yelling, threats, lashing out, avoidance, or even humor or sarcasm. These responses aren't calculated, they're instinctual. Another telltale sign is when traditional strategies don't work. That's when you know it's not about unwillingness —it's about inability.

Most importantly, these are not conscious choices. The PDA response is subconscious. When we shut down or lash out, our brains are not weighing up the pros and cons.

Ultimately, PDA reflects a chronic state of nervous system hyperarousal in response to demands, so support strategies must prioritize nervous system regulation over behavioral compliance.

What it looked like for us:

For a long time, our family didn't have the words. All we had was the pattern: Keleigh couldn't do things—even things she wanted to do. Requests, expectations, even gentle nudges could instantly trigger what looked like defiance, disrespect, or volatility. It didn't matter if it was something she enjoyed, or something simple; if it felt like a demand, it became unbearable. The more we asked, the worse it got. The more we tried to support her, the more she seemed to escalate.

At first, it just seemed like resistance. As parents, we were constantly walking a line between compassion and exhaustion, wondering why even loving, playful requests could lead to full shutdowns or explosive meltdowns. We tried charts, timers, choices, soft voices. Nothing worked for long. It was like there was a hidden tripwire—one we couldn't see, and she couldn't explain.

When that tripwire was hit, her threat response was immediate and intense. Keleigh's nervous system registers our requests not as guidance, but as danger. One thing about Keleigh: her survival skills are incredibly strong. When she felt cornered by pressure, she lashed out hard. She could take you down with a single sentence, zeroing in on your most vulnerable spot with uncanny precision. It wasn't planned or deliberately cruel. It was instinct. Her body and brain were trying to equalize the threat, and they did it with whatever tools she had in the moment—sharp words, refusal, chaos.

It was mind-boggling, especially when the trigger was something small—like brushing teeth or getting dressed. It made no logical sense. Not even after reading all those parenting books, Googling everything you can imagine, and cycling through countless therapists. None of it explained what we were living through, until we found the language for PDA.

What it feels like:

While most of my experience with PDA has been through parenting, I know now that it lives in me too. Looking back, I think it's part of why I always found work so hard—just the *expectation* to perform, respond, or engage would send my system into quiet panic. I've had an extremely exaggerated startle response for as long as I can remember, and I now see that, too, as part of my PDA profile—my nervous system constantly braced for intrusion or demand.

One of the things I've hated most is how quickly and sharply I can respond to even the gentlest requests from people I love. And the hardest part is that you don't know why. When no one ever talks about this trait, you're left to assume you're mean, cold, or harsh. You *know* it doesn't make sense to snap at someone over a simple question. But without the framework, all you have is guilt, confusion, and the silent shame of not being able to explain your own reactions.

Motherhood has been hard. Children, by nature, are demand heavy. Even when I'm resourced, their constant needs quickly drain me. When you add in Keleigh's PDA, it's like a nonstop relational puzzle layered over a brain that already struggles with relationships at baseline. It's not about love or willingness, it's about capacity. When capacity is gone, there's no pushing through. There's just system overload.

What doesn't help:

Almost everything that's typically recommended for "defiance."

Rewards, consequences, sticker charts, behavior plans, escalating authority—they all backfire. They don't reduce the behaviors, they ramp up the threats.

When someone's system is in full-blown panic, no amount of logic or incentive is going to reach them. They're not refusing because they don't want to cooperate. They're refusing because their brain has sounded the alarm: this is not safe.

What also doesn't help is being told we're manipulating, disrespectful, lazy, or spoiled. That only adds layers of shame and misunderstanding to an already overwhelmed system, and it teaches everyone involved to respond to trauma with punishment.

For parents like us, what doesn't help is hearing we're not "firm enough," or that we're letting our child "get away with things." The world doesn't understand how hard we're trying —or how much effort it takes just to avoid constant escalation.

For those of us who live with PDA, it doesn't help to be told to "just do it," or have sudden demands sprung on us, or be expected to power through without explanation. Pressure and urgency feel like someone grabbing the steering wheel from inside our chest. We need space, not force.

The hardest part is that these responses are often misread. Our freeze response looks like disrespect. Our refusal looks like rebellion. Our shutdowns look like not caring. But underneath it all is a nervous system screaming for relief. If that's not understood, things only spiral further for everyone involved.

What Does Help:

Dropping the idea that PDA has to be "fixed." It isn't a behavior problem—it's a nervous system pattern. The goal isn't compliance. It's safety, regulation, and trust.

Slowing down is incredibly helpful. Giving space. Offering options, not instructions. Letting the person with PDA feel in control—not as a manipulation tactic, but because autonomy is their oxygen. Without it, they can't breathe, let alone function.

Get curious instead of being reactive. When you see avoidance or shutdown or lashing out, ask yourself: *What demand just got triggered? What might they be afraid of?* That mindset shift changes everything.

Reduce demands wherever possible—big ones and small ones. When a demand is necessary, wrapping it in softness, humor, and relational connection can lower the perceived threat. Saying, "Want to race me to the sink?" lands very differently than "Go brush your teeth."

Allow *non-linear* paths forward. People with PDA often find sideways or creative routes through things—they may script, stall, joke, sing, or turn the demand into a game. These aren't distractions. They're regulation strategies.

Don't take it personally. That's a hard one, especially as a parent. But the lashing out isn't about us—it's about the pressure. If we can stay grounded, we become their safety net, not another source of fear. We're not doing it wrong. We're dealing with something incredibly complex. When we show up with softness and learn how to live in a relationship with PDA rather than against it, everything shifts.

Accommodations:

- Lower overall demand levels. Reduce unnecessary requests, especially during times of stress, transition, or dysregulation. Less is often more. For some folks, and in some situations, that alone may be enough to prevent overload. But when the oven knob is already turned up high—like it often is for Keleigh—you have to get creative, even with demands that seem non-negotiable. I never imagined one of my children might not finish high school in a traditional way, and I didn't picture myself being okay with that. But here we are. Keleigh is now accessing school online, and even that can sometimes be more than her system can handle. Reducing demands doesn't mean lowering expectations—it means shifting how we meet needs in a way that honors capacity.
- Offer choices, not directives. Asking "Would you rather brush your teeth before or after the show?" gives a sense of autonomy, which is everything for someone with PDA. But even this can backfire. When the PDA system is turned up, any phrasing—no matter how well-intentioned—can still feel like a demand. Use with care and be prepared to shift course if it's not landing well.
- Use indirect language. Gentle phrasing like "I wonder if…" or "I'm trying to decide when to start dinner…" can help reduce pressure, but again, only if it's truly non-coercive. Without practice and self-awareness, even these can carry an invisible push, especially if we're unconsciously using them to steer someone toward a desired outcome. Old relational habits die hard, and folks with PDA can sense subtle pressure a mile away.

When in doubt, back off, soften further, or just give space.
- Speak in declarative language. Sharing your own thoughts, plans, or observations—instead of issuing commands or asking multiple questions—can significantly reduce perceived pressure. It shifts the energy from demand to invitation, which makes all the difference in a PDA household.

A real-life example from our house: grilled cheese. Before I understood this, I used to ask Keleigh a string of questions: "Are you hungry? Do you want a grilled cheese? Pickle? Chips? What do you want to drink? Want a cookie too?" I thought I was being helpful and thorough. But it was demand after demand after demand. Her system would flip into full threat response mode (think extreme explosive words and actions), and I'd be standing there going, "I'm just trying to make you lunch!" Now? I just make the plate—grilled cheese, chips, a pickle, something sweet, and a glass of ice water—and I say, *"There's a grilled cheese in here."* The end. No decisions. No pressure. It's amazing how much smoother things go when I approach it this way. She's FAR less likely to have her threat response activated, and I'm far less likely to get caught in an hours-long meltdown over a sandwich.

Note: This is hard. It takes time to rewire how we speak and relate, especially when most of us were raised in systems where compliance was expected, and demands were the norm. It's okay if you don't always get it right. What matters most is the willingness to learn, repair, and keep showing up with curiosity and

compassion. Even small shifts in tone or phrasing can make a world of difference—and our children *feel* that effort, even when words still fall flat.

- Give time and space. Delayed processing is real, so don't expect immediate responses. Let silence be okay. This one can be hard—especially for those of us who usually feel confused and ask a lot of clarifying questions to make sense of things. But pressing for answers or resolution before a PDA nervous system has had time to settle often backfires. When we allow silence, pause, and open-ended space, it builds trust and gives everyone the breathing room they need to safely re-engage.
- Invite collaboration. Ask, "how can we make this work together?" instead of laying out a rigid plan. Shared control helps regulate the nervous system. If you try this and still meet a threat response, wait. Sometimes just offering the invitation plants a seed. You're not demanding immediate germination—you're creating the conditions for growth, when and if they're ready.
- Use humor, play, and creativity. Making things fun or silly can sometimes bypass the threat response. A song, a funny voice, or a well-timed joke can go farther than a reminder. This one is tricky though—especially once the nervous system is already activated. It's usually most effective before the demand fully registers as a threat. It's not about making light of real distress; it's about offering a side door when the front one is barricaded. It takes practice, and honestly, it's an art form. It may come more naturally with younger

children, but with time, trust, and the right rhythm, it can work even with older children and adults.
- **Avoid power struggles.** If it's turning into a tug-of-war, pause. Connection matters more than compliance. None of these accommodations are easy or natural—especially this one. The PDA brain often seeks a power struggle as a way to equalize the internal pressure, and it can be incredibly hard not to take the bait. It takes time, patience, and a paradigm shift to respond with grace and presence instead of logic, your own agenda, or a need to "win." But just knowing what's really happening beneath the surface—that this isn't manipulation, but a nervous system trying to protect itself—can go a long way.
- **Allow alternative ways to participate.** If a task feels too big, look for smaller or adjacent roles—this approach can work magic. With Keleigh, Linda is the expert in this. Going out to eat often involves too many demands and sensory challenges, but riding along and waiting in the car while we pick up takeout is one of her *favorite* things. She doesn't usually want to go into the grocery store, but she'll happily ride with me, help make the list in the car, and then help load and unload the groceries at home. When a demand is too much, Linda gets curious and creative and finds ways for Keleigh to still feel included on her own terms.
- Honor refusals. If someone says no, resist the urge to push. The ability to safely say no is part of healing. This one is *so* hard for those of us raised on compliance—truly, deeply hard. But it's also incredibly powerful. When you hear someone's no and genuinely honor it, the dynamic changes into building trust and respect. Over time, internal resources can be strengthened

because they know their voice matters and they don't have to fight to be heard.
- Regulate first. Then try again. If a demand triggers a spiral, drop it, and focus on calming down. If necessary, circle back later. Knowing what regulates you or your child is monumental. For Keleigh, it's food—especially dopamine-rich comfort food—plus her own space, and either rap music or one of her favorite shows. She needs these things like she needs air to breathe. For me, it's a long hot bath, a sudoku puzzle, and a glass of organic orange juice (yes, I'm bougie about my OJ). But seriously, knowing your go-to regulators helps immeasurably.
- Know the signs of demand fatigue. Irritability, silliness, shutdowns, and "rude" responses are often signs that the tank is running on empty. Noticing these cues—and responding accordingly—is crucial. It's not about discipline, it's about recognizing that the nervous system is overloaded and needs relief, not more pressure.
- Plan for decompression. After any high-demand day, schedule downtime. The crash is real. This is another crucial piece of the puzzle—don't treat it like a luxury or an afterthought. Schedule it in like you would anything else that matters. If you have PDA and live in this world, decompression isn't optional—it's part of the survival strategy. Without it, the system stays overloaded, and that just makes the next demand even harder to meet.
- Avoid traditional reward/punishment systems. They often increase pressure and backfire. Relationships regulate more than sticker charts ever will. In fact, sticker charts and token systems might be the *worst*

advice you could give for a PDA system (in my opinion). They pile on pressure, create shame when the demand can't be met, and damage trust. So what does work? Connection. Co-regulation. Feeling seen and safe. These are the things that build capacity—not gold stars.

- Support relationships over routines. PDA thrives on connection. If you must choose between a completed task or preserving trust, choose trust. Every time. This isn't just a preference—it's a lifeline. Trust is the only lasting foundation. If you break it to get the task done, you might win the battle, but you'll lose the war. When connection comes first, everything else becomes more possible.

A Final Note on Accommodations:

These aren't just strategies, they're full-on paradigm shifts. If this feels hard, it's because it *is* hard. Most of us were raised in systems that prioritized compliance over connection, control over collaboration. Undoing that conditioning takes time, reflection, and a whole lot of grace—for our children *and* for ourselves. You won't do it perfectly, and that's okay. This is about progress, not perfection.

One thing I hear a lot is: "But what about the real world? Aren't we just babying them?" and I get it. From the outside, these accommodations can look like coddling. But the truth is, we're not shielding our children from the world—we're equipping them for it. When we create safety, we expand capacity. When we meet their nervous system where it's at, we give it the chance to stabilize, to grow, to eventually take on more. Pushing doesn't build resilience—healthy relationships do.

Perhaps most importantly: when someone feels safe, they begin to trust themselves. These tools, this understanding— they provide people with the ability to advocate for their needs and to navigate the world. I can't help but think how different things might have been for me if I'd known these things sooner. Giving someone the language, the framework, and the felt experience of safety isn't about making life easy—it's about making life *possible*.

Radical Acceptance:

For me, radical acceptance looks like *letting go of the version of parenting I thought I had to achieve.* It means releasing the pressure of "normal" and instead leaning into the truth of who Keleigh is—and who I am, too. It means saying no to things that didn't work for us: award ceremonies, traditional classrooms, even family outings. Not because I don't care, but because I care enough to stop pushing our nervous systems to breaking point.

It means repeatedly adjusting and reshaping my expectations, not lowering them. Understanding that if Keleigh's screaming over brushing her teeth, something deeper is happening—and my job is to *see that,* not punish it.

It means learning that her "no" doesn't mean disrespect, and my "yes" doesn't mean weakness.

It meant stopping the battle I was having in my head between the parent I thought I should be and the parent Keleigh needs.

And it means doing the same for myself. Accepting that I am deeply affected by demands too. That I'm not broken, lazy or mean. That, like her, I sometimes freeze under pressure. Radical acceptance means letting myself build a life that works for my brain and body—not a performative version that mimics "success."

One of the most radical acts of acceptance for me was realizing that just because I didn't grow up with this kind of support doesn't mean I have to withhold it now. Giving Keleigh tools, compassion, and permission to be who she is doesn't mean I'm babying her. It means I'm helping her build a future where she can advocate for herself, navigate in ways that honor her truth, and thrive in a world I barely survived. That is the deepest kind of repair work I know.

Proprioception Challenges

Definition: This is our body's ability to sense where we are in space—how our limbs are positioned, how much pressure we're applying, and how we're moving through the world. It's sometimes called the "sixth sense," and it helps us with balance, coordination, and body awareness.

When someone has difficulty with proprioception, their brain doesn't always accurately interpret the body's signals. This can result in feeling disconnected from your physical self or constantly misjudging your movements. It's common in neurodivergent individuals.

Examples of Proprioceptive Challenges:

- Not knowing where your body is in space. You may frequently bump into doorframes, trip over your own feet, or misjudge how close you are to furniture.

- Applying too much or too little force. For example, you may slam a door when you meant to close it gently, or struggle to use the right pressure when writing or brushing your hair.
- Clumsiness or lack of coordination. Movements might feel awkward, ungraceful, or difficult to control, especially during physical activities like sports or dancing.
- Needing "input" to feel grounded. Some people may crave deep pressure (like weighted blankets, tight hugs, or pressing against walls) to regulate their proprioceptive system.

Rejection Sensitive Dysphoria (RSD)

Definition: Rejection Sensitive Dysphoria (RSD) is extreme emotional sensitivity and pain triggered by perceived rejection, criticism, or disappointment—whether from others or from within. It's not just about being hurt by harsh words; RSD can be activated by even gentle feedback, feeling like you've let someone down, falling short of your own standards, or experiencing any kind of disappointment.

It's estimated that nearly 100% of people with ADHD experience RSD to some degree, though it often goes unrecognized or is misdiagnosed as a mood disorder.

For someone with RSD, the emotional reaction can be immediate, overwhelming, and consuming. It may show up as:

- Sudden rage or panic
- Depressive spirals or suicidal ideation

- Illogical or intense defensiveness
- Shame so deep it feels physically painful
- A full fight, flight, or freeze response, even when the trigger seems "minor" to others

RSD often mimics other mental health conditions, but its root lies in the nervous system and how it processes threat and belonging. It's a survival-level reaction to perceived social danger as our brains interpret rejection or criticism as abandonment, failure, or loss of safety.

RSD is neurologically based and often made worse by past invalidation or trauma, and rarely discussed in the mainstream.

Rejection *perception* dysphoria isn't simply a fear of rejection, but a misinterpretation of neutral things as rejection.

What it feels like:

I spent most of my life believing I was overly sensitive. That was the story I was told—and eventually, the one I told myself. I was "too much," "too reactive," or "too hurt" by things that didn't seem to affect others in the same way. Even small disappointments or misunderstandings felt like deep emotional injuries. I didn't have the words for what was happening.

When Linda and I began having disagreements—first about how to help Keleigh, and eventually about all kinds of things—my nervous system didn't respond with fight or flight, it froze. I would almost instantly dissociate. One comment or facial expression that suggested I was falling short, and I was *gone*. I wouldn't just check out for a few minutes. I could disappear inside myself for hours or even days.

As a result, a deeply confusing pattern emerged in our relationship. I couldn't remember entire conversations, sometimes even entire stretches of time. Linda felt like I was manipulating her—rewriting events or denying things I'd said. I felt like she was putting words in my mouth or overreacting. It was maddening for both of us. Eventually, we understood that neither of us was doing it on purpose, but we couldn't make sense of what was actually happening.

Eventually, I realized I was dissociating. I tried the standard stuff—grounding techniques, therapy, mindfulness exercises—but nothing shifted. It wasn't until I stumbled across the concept of RSD that everything finally clicked.

These days, I can usually keep myself from dissociating. But honestly? That's not even the real goal. The goal is understanding and compassion. Being able to *name* what's happening and be met with support instead of confusion or escalation.

Recently, something triggered my RSD. In the past, that would have meant a total spiral—freeze, dissociation, memory gaps, and days of feeling broken. But this time, something different happened. I was able to say the words out loud: *"I'm experiencing RSD."*

That moment was years in the making. Years of learning, unlearning, trying to notice my patterns, trying to separate myself from the shame that always followed. It didn't happen overnight, but when it happened, it was transformative.

Linda responded immediately. *"This isn't rejection. It's not even personal."* Even though her words didn't stop the RSD from happening—because it's neurological, not logical—it changed everything.

I still needed space, and not just a few minutes behind a closed door. My preferred accommodation is to truly be alone so the storm can pass through me without interference. This time, I was able to do that. Linda understood—I wasn't accused of being dramatic or distant. She didn't try to fix it, talk me out of it, she just gave me the support I needed.

The result? No spiral. No dissociation. No memory loss. No "you said/I said" aftermath that left us both reeling. Just clarity, love, and understanding. It felt like a miracle.

I'm not totally free from dissociation, but it's so much less frequent now. The reason isn't that I've conquered RSD, it's that I understand it. I have language. Most importantly, I have a partner who knows that what looks irrational from the outside is actually a deep neurological pattern being activated, and who meets that pattern with grace.

Now, I recognize the onset of RSD more clearly, but that doesn't mean it hurts any less. For me, RSD feels like a violent storm that crashes into me from nowhere. One moment I'm fine, and the next I'm completely drenched in sheer horror—like I've done something terribly wrong or *am* something wrong. I know it isn't logical. I know it's not about actual rejection. But the storm doesn't care about logic. It comes fast, floods everything, and clings to me like a second skin. No amount of reasoning can part the clouds until it's run its course.

What doesn't help:

RSD is not a behavior problem. It's not an overreaction, a character flaw, or a sign of immaturity. But because it can look confusing from the outside, people often reach for the wrong tools—logic, pep talks, criticism, correction, even gentle reasoning—and all of it tends to backfire. Telling someone they're overreacting doesn't calm them down, it confirms the exact fear RSD planted: that their feelings are too much, that *they* are too much. Asking someone to explain why they feel this way only deepens the spiral. Often, they don't know why—they only know they're in pain. Being asked to justify that pain can make them feel even more broken. When others take it personally, the whole experience intensifies. RSD creates the feeling of having failed or hurt someone, so if the response is hurt or frustration, it validates the distorted belief of being bad or unlovable.

Attempts to fix it, even well-meaning ones, often increase shame. What's needed is understanding, space, and nervous system regulation. When someone with RSD is pushed to stay present or talk things through before they're ready, their system may default to a fight, flight, or freeze response. It's not avoidance or defiance—it's protection.

What does help:

Real, grounded understanding starts with having the language to name what's happening. Being able to say, "I'm experiencing RSD," or saying to your child, "This could be RSD," gives a framework for understanding—something many of us were never given. It turns what used to feel like personal failure into something that's neurologically explainable, something that can be supported instead of judged. In these moments, validation is powerful—being believed goes a long way. When someone meets me with presence instead of pressure, it eases the shame and lets the storm move through.

For many of us, the most helpful thing is nonjudgmental space to let the emotional wave pass. That doesn't mean withdrawing in anger or avoidance—it's about protection, regulation, and returning when we're ready. What helps isn't fixing or dissecting, but gentleness, respect, and knowing that we're doing the best we can. The people who respond this way are the ones we can trust. Over time, those safe experiences become internalized, and they help us navigate future spirals with more self-awareness and less collapse. It doesn't make RSD go away, but it makes it survivable and less lonely.

Accommodations:

- Use language that validates, not minimizes. Say things like, "This feels really big right now, and that's okay," or "I believe you." Validation eases the nervous system and can prevent escalation.
- Name the experience without shame. Gently offer language like, "I wonder if this might be RSD?" so it becomes something to understand, not something to hide.
- Don't force explanations. Avoid immediately asking, "Why are you upset?" or "What triggered this?" RSD often isn't logical, so pushing for clarity too soon can deepen the distress.
- Give space without punishment. If they need to leave the room, take a walk, or stop the conversation, let them. Space is not avoidance—it's a regulation strategy.

- Avoid taking things personally. Even when the reaction seems directed at you, remind yourself (and maybe them, later) that it's about their wiring, not your worth.
- Stay calm and consistent. A calm presence can anchor someone in emotional free fall. Avoid reacting with intensity, even if the RSD expression feels disproportionate.
- Use visual cues or gentle reminders afterward. A written note, a soft "Are you okay now?", or a comforting routine can help reestablish connection without pressure.
- Avoid public corrections or critiques. Even neutral feedback can trigger a shame spiral. Save sensitive conversations for private, low-stakes moments.
- **Normalize dysregulation.** Talk openly about how emotions can sometimes feel overwhelming, and that everyone deserves support while learning how to navigate them.

Radical Acceptance:

For most of my life, I thought I was "too sensitive," "too reactive," and "too emotional." I didn't have the words for RSD; I just knew that I felt things way too deeply, and that the pain of disappointing someone or feeling misunderstood could take me out for days. When that pain led to behaviors people didn't understand—like dissociation, shutting down, crying over "nothing," or panicking over a text message—I assumed it was a personal failure.

Radical acceptance changed that. Slowly. Unevenly. But completely.

I still experience RSD, and it's horrible when it hits. But now I know it's a nervous system reaction rooted in how my brain processes rejection or perceived rejection. It's not immaturity, drama, or manipulation.

Radical acceptance means knowing I can't logic myself out of RSD, but I *can* build safety around it. I can have a partner who meets my spirals with grace, not judgment. I can step away without guilt, regulate in the ways I've learned that work for me, and come back when I'm ready. I can name it out loud and be met with compassion, not confusion. And I can now offer this same acceptance to my daughter. I can help her understand that her own stormy feelings aren't bad or wrong. That she's not too much or unlovable. She's just wired differently, and she deserves to be supported in that wiring, not punished.

Radical acceptance doesn't mean giving up or letting things slide. It means recognizing that healing doesn't come from force or shame. It means I get to live my life with more clarity and less collapse, and so does my daughter. Honestly, that feels like the most beautiful, radical thing I could ever offer her or myself.

Routine

The need for routine refers to the strong internal drive many neurodivergent people have for structure, predictability, and sameness in daily life. Routines offer a sense of safety, reduce anxiety, and help manage the constant overwhelm that accompanies a fast-paced, sensory-heavy, and socially confusing world.

For autistic people, routines are often essential for regulation. They provide anchors that help us feel oriented in space and time. When routines are disrupted, it can trigger disorientation, shutdowns, or meltdowns — not because we're inflexible, but because our systems depend on predictability to function.

For people with ADHD, however, novelty and flexibility are just as essential. ADHD brains crave stimulation and may resist or become bored of repetitive structure. The need for spontaneity and variety can clash dramatically with a need for routine—especially when someone is both ADHD and autistic.

This can cause an internal tug-of-war, which can be exhausting and deeply confusing— especially when others don't understand the invisible labor of managing this conflict. Understanding this trait and how differently it can show up across neurotypes is key to building supportive systems.

Sensory Processing Differences (SPD)

Sensory Processing Differences (SPD) refers to a neurological difference in which the brain has difficulty receiving, organizing, or responding appropriately to sensory input. This can involve any of the senses as well as balance (vestibular), body awareness (proprioception), or internal bodily sensations (interoception).

People with SPD may be hypersensitive (over-responsive), hyposensitive (under-responsive), or a fluctuating mix of both.

These challenges can affect how someone regulates their emotions, navigates daily environments, and engages in social or functional tasks.

Related terms:

- **Tactile defensiveness**: An aversion to touch that can make clothing, tags, grooming, or physical contact feel irritating or even painful. (Real life example: For about ten solid years, there were moments when Linda would lovingly rub my back or legs, and I felt like I was dying. Not metaphorically. Like actual nervous system agony. But instead of saying anything, I'd casually reposition myself or suddenly remember something I *had* to get up and do. I never mentioned how awful it felt until a full decade later. When I finally told her, she looked at me like I had grown a second head. "What the hell?! Why didn't you tell me that?" Ten years?" I didn't even have the words for it. I didn't realize it was a thing. I just thought I was weird.
- **Vestibular sensitivity**: Discomfort or distress with movement or changes in head position, often resulting in motion sickness or balance issues.
- **Sensory seeking**: A strong craving for sensory input, which may include constant movement, touching everything, making loud noises, or seeking out strong tastes, smells, or physical sensations.

What It Feels Like:

For me, sensory processing differences —what was formally called Sensory Processing Disorder—have always been a part of my experience. I have extreme sensitivities to noise and light. Bright lights feel like knives behind my eyes. Sudden or overlapping sounds send my nervous system into full alert. Crowded spaces, loud music, echoey rooms, fluorescent lighting—they can undo me within minutes. And it's not something I "get used to" over time. My system doesn't adapt. It endures.

Keleigh was diagnosed with SPD at a very young age by an occupational therapist. She was clearly overwhelmed by sensory input such as sounds, textures, and movement, and struggled to regulate herself. But somehow, despite how clearly she was showing signs of a dysregulated sensory system, that diagnosis didn't raise any additional red flags. No one suggested we look deeper. No one said, "Hey, this might be part of something bigger." It's interesting—and deeply frustrating—how often our systems catch the pieces but fail to connect them. SPD was treated as something Keleigh might "grow out of," or something we could "manage," rather than as a signal that her nervous system processes the world differently.

It's like living in a body that is constantly startled, overloaded, or flooded by things that other people barely register. When no one connects the dots—and we don't have the language to connect them—we are set up as failures. Naming it is the first step to acceptance and support.

What Doesn't Help:

The "just deal with it" approach of pushing through doesn't work. In fact, exposure without support, pressure to stay in overstimulating places, or insisting that someone "get used to it" often backfires. It can lead to shutdowns, meltdowns, or deep emotional dysregulation. It also doesn't help to dismiss sensory needs as picky, dramatic, controlling, or attention-seeking. Sensory overload is not a behavior issue—it's a full-body experience. Ignoring it doesn't make it go away; it just teaches the person to suffer silently and hide it better, which only compounds stress. Trying to force a child to tolerate a sensory environment before they're ready—even if it's something "fun"—tends to result in disconnection and conflict. And it certainly doesn't help to assume they'll eventually grow out of it, typically, they just learn to mask or avoid entirely.

What Does Help:

Starting from a place of trust is vital, so believe someone when they say something is too loud, too bright, too itchy, too cold. Adjust the environment instead of asking the person to endure it. This might mean dimming lights, turning off background music, skipping the crowded restaurant, or simply offering noise-canceling headphones without judgment. It helps to provide alternatives that still allow participation—like letting someone wait in the car, order takeout, or choose their own clothing textures. It also helps to let go of the "shoulds" —what they should be able to handle, what should be fun, what should be tolerable—and replace them with curiosity and compassion.

Sometimes, life will call for moments that you know will be a sensory nightmare, such as travel days, holidays, appointments, or group events that just can't be avoided. In those moments, the most helpful thing to do is plan ahead: make every possible accommodation *beforehand,* and just as importantly, build in breaks and recovery time *afterward.* We all need space to recalibrate, and for people with sensory processing differences, that space can be the difference between burnout and balance.

Accommodations:

- Noise-canceling headphones or earplugs for overwhelming environments (schools, stores, events, etc.). I couldn't believe how much these helped me when I first got them; they really are worth the investment!
- Control over lighting. Use of natural light and lamps instead of overhead fluorescent lighting, with dimmable options where possible (candles are one of my favorites!)
- Quiet spaces or sensory break areas allow a designated place to retreat when overstimulated, even for a few minutes
- Permission to opt out of overstimulating settings (assemblies, crowded cafeterias, group work, certain social events) without penalty
- Use of sensory aids such as weighted blankets, compression clothing, fidgets, or chewable jewelry for grounding
- Reduced exposure to overlapping sounds (music, talking, background noise), for example, asking to turn off background music during work or study
- Predictable routines and advance notice of changes reduce anxiety caused by sensory unpredictability
- Freedom to wear preferred fabrics and clothing allow for comfort over dress codes or norms
- Flexible seating or movement options such as standing desks, rocking chairs, wobble cushions, or the freedom to move/stretch as needed
- Avoidance of scented products or cleaning chemicals in shared spaces, or allowing use of scent-free alternatives

- Modified classroom or workplace tasks to account for sensory overwhelm (e.g., doing presentations one-on-one instead of in front of the group)
- Respect and validation when sensory overload occurs, which means no punishment, shaming, or forcing someone to push through

Radical Acceptance:

For me, radical acceptance of my sensory processing differences looks like living in a house without overhead lighting. I use lamps with 25-watt bulbs, and I only switch them on when absolutely needed. In the predawn hours, I light candles—not because I'm being poetic (though it *is* kind of poetic), but because it's what my nervous system needs to feel safe and soft. I carry my earplugs in my purse at all times—they're lifesavers in stores, restaurants, or anywhere the world gets too loud, too fast. I also have a major sensory issue with cold, especially air conditioning. Traveling is hard on me, so I've learned to come prepared. I always bring an eye mask, earplugs or AirPods, warm clothes, and cozy socks. If I know I'll be somewhere with air conditioning, I make sure to have a sweater or blanket with me. I've just accepted that I need those things to stay regulated.

I have so many sensory accommodations in place, I don't always notice them—they've just become *my way of life*. I only realize how many I rely on when I leave my home environment and suddenly can't find the quiet, warmth, and softness I've built around me. That's the thing about radical acceptance—it's not about fixing the trait. Instead, it's about *working with it*, building a life around your real needs instead of constantly forcing yourself to endure what everyone else finds tolerable. This is how I live now—not because I'm fragile, but because I finally know what I need.

I've also had to learn what radical acceptance looks like as the parent of a child with SPD. Keleigh gets completely overwhelmed in public spaces such as stores, restaurants, and amusement parks. Like many parents, we tried to make things work because they were supposed to be "fun" or "normal." But over time, we learned that pushing through only led to stress, meltdowns, and disappointment for everyone. Now, we try to support her exactly where she is. For example, one of her absolute favorite things to do is ride along with us but stay in the car. The car is her safe space. Wherever we are going, she enjoys having full control of the music, a show on her phone, and full control of the temperature. When we go out to eat, she comes for the ride. We order takeout for her at the same time we order our food. When the food's ready, we bring hers to her in the car, and we eat ours inside. She's happy, we're happy, and everyone leaves with full bellies—no bargaining, no tears, no one left behind. It's not what we imagined restaurant outings would look like, but it works. More importantly, *it honors her*.

Clothes shopping has also been a major challenge. She often gets overwhelmed in stores but also gets frustrated at home that she doesn't have what she needs. When she's overwhelmed, she—seemingly subconsciously—gets so close to us that she's quite literally walking *on* us. It used to frustrate us, but now we recognize it for what it is: a stress response, a sign that her system is maxed out. On a recent trip, she left the store. Instead of chasing her or trying to talk her through it in the moment, I let her go to the car, and I kept shopping. I picked out some options I thought she might like, then FaceTimed her from the store to show her a pared-down selection. From the quiet comfort of the car, she was able to choose clothes that worked for her. She got what she needed without the overload, and that, to me, is a win.

Radical acceptance means we no longer expect her to fit into unmanageable systems. We adapt and pivot, and in doing so, we suffer less and love more.

Sleep Irregularities

For neurodivergent people, sleep is often anything but straightforward. Many of us struggle to fall asleep, stay asleep, or wake up feeling rested. Some live on a delayed sleep cycle (like falling asleep at 2 a.m. and waking at 10 a.m.), while others experience insomnia, nighttime overstimulation, or frequent waking. These aren't bad habits—our brains are often wired differently when it comes to sleep regulation.

Research shows that melatonin production and delivery is often awry in autistic and ADHD brains. Our internal clocks may be delayed, irregular, or simply out of sync with the world's 9-to-5 expectations. This biological mismatch can make "fixing" sleep much more complex than just turning off screens or going to bed earlier.

The result? Chronic exhaustion, trouble with routines, and even more dysregulation—because everything is harder when you're running on empty. It's a cycle that feeds itself.

Accommodations can include flexible schedules, low-demand mornings, dim lighting in the evening, sensory-friendly bedding, using sleep aids like melatonin (when appropriate), and recognizing that late-night productivity or irregular hours might not be flaws—they might be our natural rhythm.

Social-Relational Layers

There are a few other traits that often show up under the umbrella of neurodivergent social challenges that might not need full sections, but they're worth naming, especially because they can be incredibly confusing in relationships if no one understands what's happening.

Difficulty with **conversational rhythms**, where someone may unintentionally dominate a conversation or never think to ask others about themselves, can cause problems. It's not out of selfishness, but because our brains aren't wired to automatically track those back-and-forth social "rules."

Alternating between total silence and non-stop talking is another issue, and it is just as disorienting for others. It's not about being hot and cold, it's about whether the words are immediately accessible.

Literal thinking can also impact how we interpret language. Jokes, sarcasm, or subtle hints may go completely over our heads—or be taken at face value.

Then there are **eye contact differences**: some ND people avoid eye contact completely; in my case, I learned early on that I *should* make eye contact, so I developed a deeply ingrained habit of staring directly into people's eyes without blinking, because I thought that's what good listening looked like. People still call me out on it, and I still don't really know what else to do.

You might also see things like **flat or exaggerated facial expressions**, depending on how someone regulates their emotions, interprets social context, or manages their internal resources at any given moment.

Emotional mirroring is where we unconsciously mimic others' energy, mood, or gestures—not because we're being inauthentic, but because it helps us understand what's happening in a situation or connect to what the other person is feeling.

Info-dumping or monologuing is another common trait— sharing deep, passionate knowledge about something we care about without realizing others might be overwhelmed, bored, or trying to change the subject. Similarly, **misreading tone or social vibes** can lead to big misunderstandings. We may assume someone is angry when they're not, or completely miss that someone *is* upset, because we're not intuitively reading their emotional cues.

And don't forget: these traits are usually not happening in isolation—they're all working at the same time, layered and overlapping, often in conjunction with other traits like Auditory Processing Disorder and Rejection Sensitive Dysphoria (RSD). It's not one challenge, it's an interconnected system of how we experience and interpret the social world.

Special Interest

Definition: For a neurodivergent person, a special interest is a deeply meaningful, intense, highly focused passion or area of fascination, especially common among autistic individuals. Special interests often involve deep dives into a particular subject, topic, activity, or theme, sometimes lasting for years and sometimes shifting over time. These interests aren't simply hobbies—they can be joyful obsessions, regulation tools, learning gateways, and sources of identity or comfort.

What It Feels Like:

For a while, one of my special interests was self-help. I devoured books, podcasts, and articles—anything I could get my hands on. I wasn't just curious; I was *driven* to understand myself, and figure out how to survive and grow. These days, two of my go-to special interests are Sudoku puzzles and the news. It might sound like an odd mix, but both give my brain something structured and immersive to hold onto, and they feel like mine. I engage with these interests daily, not as forms of escapism, but because they help me stay regulated. They bring order to chaos. They help me transition. They offer comfort when everything else feels too loud or unpredictable. When I'm enjoying these interests, I feel like I'm letting my nervous system rest inside something it loves. It's not a waste of time or indulgence. It's medicine—and honoring that has made a huge difference in how I care for myself.

Accommodations:

- Make time and space for special interests without guilt—they aren't distractions; they're often vital tools for regulation and focus

- Allow special interests to be integrated into learning, work, or therapy whenever possible—they can enhance motivation, engagement, and comprehension
- Provide freedom to engage with certain special interests during breaks or downtime, as a way to self-regulate (e.g., puzzles, reading, researching, listening to podcasts)
- Avoid pathologizing or shaming the depth or intensity of a special interest—what might seem "too much" to others is often just right for a neurodivergent brain
- Recognize the importance of repetition and consistency—returning to the same interest daily or even hourly can be part of what makes it grounding
- Support creative or non-traditional expressions of special interests, such as stimming while talking about them, scripting, or info-dumping
- Offer alternatives to social situations that compete with or interfere with special interest time, especially during times of stress or dysregulation
- Give access to tools and materials that support the interest—whether that's books, puzzles, tech, craft supplies, or time alone
- Let special interests be a social bridge, when possible, but don't force it— sometimes they're private, and that's okay
- Support transitions out of special interest time with gentleness and clear cues, especially for younger folk, or those with PDA or ADHD profiles

Spiky Skills

Definition: "Spiky skills" refer to a cognitive or functional profile where a person has very high abilities in some areas and significant challenges in others, rather than an even or flat set of skills. This is especially common in neurodivergent individuals, including those with autism, ADHD, dyslexia, and other forms of neurodivergence.

Unlike the neurotypical expectation of consistent performance across different domains, spiky profiles may look like:
- A child who reads at a college level but can't tie their shoes.
- An adult who gives brilliant presentations but forgets to eat lunch or pay bills.
- Someone who can solve complex math problems but struggles with small talk or time management.

Why It Matters:
Spiky skills can be misunderstood in schools, workplaces, and relationships. People may assume someone is lazy, oppositional, or not trying in the areas where they struggle, especially if they see brilliance elsewhere. But these peaks and valleys aren't about effort, they reflect how the brain is wired. Understanding spiky profiles helps us replace judgment with support. It reminds us that strengths don't cancel out challenges, and vice versa. Both are real and important.

Stimming

Definition: (short for *self-stimulatory behavior*) refers to repetitive movements, sounds, or actions that are used by neurodivergent individuals to self-regulate emotions, manage sensory input, express excitement, or cope with overwhelm. Stimming can be physical (like hand-flapping, rocking, or pacing), auditory (like humming or repeating phrases), or visual (like watching spinning objects or lights).

What It Feels Like:

Stimming hasn't been a huge challenge for me or my daughter. We both do things like tapping, bouncing a leg, or repeating words under our breath, but it feels like our "oven knobs" for this one are turned down lower than some of the others. It's not something we've ever had to manage in a big way, so I don't have a lot of personal stories to offer. That said, I know that for many neurodivergent folks, stimming is a vital part of self-regulation—sometimes life-saving—and it deserves to be supported, not pathologized. So, while I don't speak from the deepest end of this trait, I still want to include accommodations that can make a real difference.

Accommodations:

- Allow stimming without shame—hand-flapping, rocking, fidgeting, and other repetitive behaviors should not be punished or pathologized
- Normalize the use of stim tools like chewable jewelry, textured items, fidget toys, or weighted objects
- Offer quiet corners or designated spaces where people can stim freely without feeling watched or judged
- Support movement breaks during long periods of having to sit, pacing, stretching, or bouncing can be regulation tools
- Avoid requiring eye contact, which can suppress natural stimming and increase distress

- Educate peers and staff (in schools or workplaces) so they understand stimming is a regulation tool, not a distraction or disruption
- Recognize verbal stims (like humming, repeating phrases, or scripting) as valid—offer noise-canceling headphones to others if needed, rather than asking the person to stop
- Respect sensory needs that may lead to visual or tactile stimming—such as staring at lights, spinning objects, or repetitive hand movements
- Validate stimming as communication—sometimes it's how someone expresses excitement, anxiety, or emotional overload when words don't come easily
- Offer alternative regulation options if certain stims are unsafe (like head-banging or skin picking), but do so with compassion and without eliminating stimming altogether

---

Strong Sense of Justice

Definition: This is an intense internal drive to recognize and respond to fairness, equality, and ethical treatment—both for oneself and others. People with this trait often feel deeply upset by hypocrisy, mistreatment, or broken rules and may react strongly to perceived injustice, even in situations others see as minor.

This trait can be both a gift and a challenge. It drives us to be advocates and allies, but it can also make life feel more overwhelming because we see and feel injustices so intensely.

What It Feels Like:

Having a strong sense of justice feels like carrying a fire in your chest that can't be extinguished. It burns hot when someone is mistreated, ignored, or silenced—and it doesn't settle until something is done. It's not about being "dramatic" or "too sensitive," though that's often how it is interpreted. It's a visceral, deep-in-your-gut knowing that what's happening isn't okay. For some of us, walking away from that and pretending not to notice simply isn't an option.

I remember watching a patient being completely failed by the healthcare system. I spent several days advocating for her nonstop by challenging policies, calling meetings, and pushing through resistance. My boss finally turned to me and said, "When are you going to stop bitching about this?" I looked her in the eye and said, "When we do something about it." It wasn't an act of rebellion; it was my nervous system demanding I speak up. It didn't matter if it cost me my reputation or my job. What mattered was that this woman had someone in her corner. I was always the "annoying" one, the "difficult" one, the one who wouldn't let things go. But it was never about being difficult. It was about being unable to look away.

I see the same fire in my daughter. From a young age, she couldn't stand to watch her fellow students being unfairly treated. If a teacher was dismissive, sarcastic, or controlling—especially toward children who were struggling—she would speak up loudly and relentlessly. She wouldn't let it go, even when it got her into trouble. Teachers labeled her "disruptive" or "disrespectful," and she was sent out of the classroom, suspended, or reprimanded, but she wouldn't stop. It wasn't defiance. It was that sense of justice burning inside of her, too strongly to contain. Just like me, she couldn't understand why others didn't see what she saw. She wasn't trying to be difficult. She was standing up for someone who couldn't stand up for themselves.

The trait is both a gift and a heavy weight. It makes us powerful advocates, loyal allies, and courageous truth-tellers. But it also makes life more painful. We don't just see injustice, we *feel* it. We lie awake thinking about things others forget by dinner. In this current political climate, where injustice feels like it's roaring from every corner, this part of me feels especially raw and inflamed. Sometimes I wonder what it would be like to care less, but I know that's not possible because this trait is woven into me. And while it may exhaust me at times, it also anchors me to what I believe is good and right in the world. It reminds me that silence is not an option. Even when it costs me, I will always speak up—and so will Keleigh.

Accommodation:

- Recognize that speaking up about fairness is not defiance, it's a form of advocacy often tied to deep moral reasoning
- Allow space to express concerns about perceived injustice, with time to process feelings safely (verbally, in writing, and always with a trusted adult)
- Create structured ways for students to voice concerns, such as a "justice journal," feedback box, or private check-ins
- Offer co-regulation tools for emotional intensity, especially when witnessing harm to others becomes dysregulating
- Help build language around nuance, so they can hold both their moral clarity and the complexity of systems that may not immediately change

- Model validation when they speak up—even if action isn't always possible, acknowledgment matters
- Reduce punitive consequences for respectful advocacy, and differentiate between disrespect and distress-driven insistence

Radical Acceptance:

Having a strong sense of justice is a trait that is part of us, and I no longer see it as "too much." I see it as part of my wiring and a gift. I've learned to name it out loud, both for myself and others. When I name it plainly and without shame, people often pause. They soften. They get it. Some even say, "Wait, that's a thing? That's me too." Naming it helps us all feel a little less alone—and a little more seen for the fierce, caring, justice-driven people we are.

Swiss Cheese Memory

Definition: *Swiss cheese memory* is a casual but relatable term often used in neurodivergent communities to describe memory that has noticeable holes in it, like slices of Swiss cheese. It means you might remember some things with vivid detail, while other things—even important or recent ones—just disappear.

This experience is common among people who are neurodivergent. It isn't about willful forgetfulness or not paying attention—it's about how the brain encodes, stores, and retrieves information, often in unpredictable ways.
Examples of Swiss Cheese Memory:
- Forgetting entire conversations or events that others clearly recall

- Remembering tiny, obscure details from years ago, but not where you just put your keys
- Knowing you *used to know* something, but now it's just gone
- Being accused of "conveniently forgetting," when the gaps are real (and frustrating)

It can be confusing for others and painful for us, but it's a real neurological pattern.

A Few More Cognitive and Communication Processing Differences

There are several more traits that often ride alongside the others we've covered, each one adding a layer of complexity to how neurodivergent people process and respond to the world.

- **Nonlinear Thinking**. Many neurodivergent people don't think in straight lines. Our thoughts branch, spiral, or connect like constellations. We often see patterns others miss but getting them out in a linear conversation can be tricky, because they don't always follow the expected "point A to point B" format.
- **Slow Processing Speed**. This is not a lack of intelligence. In fact, sometimes it's the opposite—there's so much happening internally, it just takes longer to respond. This is especially true when under pressure or in unfamiliar environments. We may need a longer runway before takeoff.
- **Context Blindness**. Difficulty recognizing or responding to the subtle rules of a situation. We might not know when to adjust tone, behavior, or expectations to fit a given environment, especially if those rules are unspoken. It's not about being rude or defiant —it's about not seeing the cues in the first place.

The Paradox of Being Neurodivergent

The traits of neurodivergence aren't neat or separate. They don't show up one at a time in tidy little boxes. They layer, overlap, and collide inside us—constantly shifting depending on our internal resources and external environment. One moment a trait is dialed all the way up, the next it's quiet, and then suddenly another one jumps in. It's dynamic, alive, and—honestly—confusing for everyone, including me.

It's not clear or consistent. It's full of unfathomable paradoxes for ourselves and the outside world. I experience alexithymia, the inability to name or feel emotions, and I also experience emotional dysregulation, where the emotions are too big, too fast, and too much. I miss basic social cues, but I pick up on the tiniest shifts in energy, tone, or behavior. I forget my own children exist when they are not in front of me, but I can remember exactly where I last saw a paperclip in 2003. I can't function in loud spaces, but sometimes I *need* loud music to regulate. I crave movement but forget I have a body. I can't filter sensory input, but I can hyperfocus for twelve hours straight if I fall into the right groove.

It feels all so...disorienting. Without language for this you don't know who you are. One day you're steady, competent, even vibrant. The next, it's like that version of you disappears and you can't function at all. You look back at yourself and wonder how both can be true. It makes you feel inconsistent, unreliable, like you can't even trust your own self to show up in a way that makes sense. You're never fully one thing or the other. You're both, sometimes back-to-back, often all at once.

That whiplash leaves you second-guessing your reality, doubting your identity, and carrying a quiet fear that others will see you as unstable—or worse, unworthy.

Others often perceive this paradox as flighty, confusing, weird, at best—at worst, manipulative, rude, even "a bitch." Because others can't put us in a box they can predict, their response is often harsh. And that only compounds the pain and confusion.

This is the paradox: the very wiring that makes us unique is also what makes us hard for others—and ourselves—to understand. Understanding and being able to name this concept is the first step in decreasing some of the mystery, embracing who we are and helping our support system understand us and know how to support us best.

None of it lines up. None of it follows a neat cause-and-effect formula. And yet, this *is* how my brain works. Neurodivergence doesn't follow neurotypical rules. It isn't logical in the way people expect. Our experiences often contradict themselves, sometimes within very short timespans, and that's part of what makes it so hard to explain and accommodate. When we try to describe our feelings or experiences, we can sound like we're making excuses, being inconsistent, or not trying hard enough. But we're not. It is our wiring.

It's also one reason why so many of us fly under the radar, and are misjudged, mislabeled, or misunderstood. It's why our own inner voice so often becomes cruel. We don't always understand how we can be so capable and so impaired, so aware and so disconnected, so full of emotion and so numb.

I used to often be called an enigma (polite version), or confusing (more honest), or sometimes even a less flattering version of these adjectives. I never knew how to categorize myself. Every time I took a personality quiz, or a leadership style assessment, my results were bizarre. I'd land in some unheard-of combo or contradictory corner that didn't quite fit anywhere. I was a walking paradox, and I felt as baffled by myself as everyone else did.

But now I know, it's just the way I am. The world may not know how to hold our contradictions, but that doesn't mean we can't learn to hold them ourselves.

The Weight of Being Misunderstood

One thread that stands out is the feeling of being persistently misunderstood. Not just by strangers, but by teachers, coworkers, friends, partners, and sometimes even by ourselves. We spend so much of our lives being incorrectly read: our silence mistaken for coldness, our bluntness for rudeness, our honesty for disrespect. Our confusion gets labeled as inattention. Our overwhelm interpreted as drama. And the worst part? When people don't understand us, they fill in the gaps with their own narrative, and we're the ones left holding the shame.

For many of us, this feeling started when we were young. Phrases such as "too sensitive," "talk too much," "never talk," "too intense," "too emotional," and "too much" formed feedback loops that began before we found the language to describe ourselves. We started masking, adjusting, and shrinking, trying to be more palatable and predictable. But still, the misunderstanding continued. It leaves a kind of aching grief. We aren't just trying to connect, we're also constantly trying to *repair* the connection people think we've broken, when really, they just never understood how we were wired in the first place.

The weight of being misunderstood chips away at our self-trust. We question our instincts, memories, and tone. We over-explain, over-apologize, or stop speaking up altogether. Sometimes we internalize everything so deeply, we believe we are always the problem.

The more I've come to understand my neurodivergence, the more I've been able to release some of that weight. It wasn't me failing to be understandable. It was the world failing to understand me. The more we talk openly and honestly, the more room we make for others to drop the mask too. The opposite of misunderstanding isn't just understanding —it's *being seen*.

Time Blindness

Definition: Time blindness is a neurological difficulty with perceiving, estimating, and managing the passage of time. It can affect a person's ability to sense how long tasks take, how much time has passed, or how much time remains before something needs to happen. This makes planning, transitioning, and meeting deadlines extremely challenging.

People with time blindness often:

- Feel like things either take *forever* or *no time at all*

- Lose track of time even when they *know* something important is coming up
- Over or underestimate how long a task will take
- Struggle to be on time or to stop being hyperfocused
- Experience only two modes of time: now and not now

What if feels like:

Time blindness can feel like living without an internal clock. I can check the time ten times and still miss an appointment. I set timers, reminders, and alarms, yet I still run late, forget, or get stuck in something else entirely. It's like time isn't linear; it's slippery.

Sometimes it's as if the whole day has disappeared, and I have no idea where it went. Other times, five minutes can feel like an hour. I'll glance at the clock thinking I still have plenty of time, and suddenly I'm twenty minutes late and scrambling. It makes me feel so dumb sometimes—like everyone apart from me got the manual about how to manage time. Even when I'm trying my best, I still end up feeling unreliable or irresponsible, and that internal shame can be brutal. I know I'm not lazy. I know I care, but time keeps slipping through my fingers, and I'm left feeling like a failure.

When I'm engaged in something interesting or urgent, everything else evaporates. The world shrinks to just *that one thing* until someone interrupts me, or I resurface and realize hours have passed. When something is in the future—even the near future—it doesn't feel real. My brain files it under "not now," meaning it doesn't exist until it's *right now* and suddenly very urgent.

It often feels like my brain only recognizes two times: "not now" and "right now." There's no gradual sense of something approaching—no internal countdown or natural urgency that builds as time passes. Either something is off my radar, or it suddenly feels like an emergency. I rarely experience that in-between space where people seem to calmly prepare for things. I'm either relaxed and unaware, or panicked and scrambling. My brain doesn't register time passing in a linear or intuitive way.

Planning is hard, and so are transitions. Not because I'm disorganized or defiant, but because time, as a concept, doesn't anchor itself in my mind the way it seems to for other people. I'm not avoiding things on purpose; I'm floating in an unruly timeline. It can be incredibly hard to feel trustworthy, competent, or even *functional* when your relationship to time constantly works against you.

What didn't help:

Time blindness isn't about laziness or how much you care, it's about how my brain processes time. But because it *looks* like poor planning or irresponsibility, the responses I get often make things worse. Being scolded or told to "just try harder" doesn't magically give me a sense of time—it just adds shame and frustration. Reminders laced with judgment, like "Why didn't you leave earlier?" or "You always do this" don't help me get anywhere faster, they just deepen the feeling that I'm failing at something basic.

Deadlines and countdowns with no flexibility can also flip my nervous system into panic mode. When people assume I don't care, or that I'm choosing to be late or forgetful, it's not just hurtful and inaccurate. I care *deeply*—so deeply that I often feel crushed by the weight of my own disappointment when I repeatedly get it wrong. The more pressure that's added, the harder it becomes to engage at all. Criticism, shame, and rigid expectations don't create structure for me—they create shutdown.

What does help:

Support that's rooted in compassion, not correction. I've learned that I can't *feel* time passing the way others do, so I must *externalize* it in any way I can. That's why I set endless timers—not because I'm disorganized, but because I know time will escape me, no matter how important or unmissable something is.

When I was younger, I thought I could train myself out of time blindness. I'd think, "There's no way I'll forget something this important," or "This is such a big deal, I'll definitely remember the time." But I wouldn't. Over and over, time would just... slip. So now, I work with my brain instead of against it. If I need to be somewhere, I'll set a timer an hour before, 20 minutes before, 5 minutes before, and again at the actual time I need to leave. I even have daily timers just to give me a sense of where I am in the day—without them, hours can pass without me even noticing.

Visual timers, calendars, and sensory anchors like music or routines can also help me track the flow of time in a more embodied way. But one of the most helpful things is simply having people in my life who believe me when I say this is real. It's not laziness or carelessness—it's how my brain is wired. Having that understanding (and flexibility) from others reduces the panic and shame I carry, and it gives me the chance to show up with more confidence and consistency.

Accommodations:

- Use multiple alarms and timers for key transitions—when to get ready, when to leave, when to take a break, etc. (Think: reminders *before* the thing, not just at the time of the thing.)
- Set recurring daily timers to help anchor your sense of where you are in the day (e.g., one at 10am, 2pm, and 6pm—even if nothing specific is happening at those times).
- Break tasks into timed chunks using techniques like the Pomodoro method (e.g., 25 minutes on, 5 minutes off) to create external time structure.
- Use visual time tools, like analog clocks, color-coded calendars, or visual timers (like Time Timer). This is especially good for children or visual learners.
- Build in buffer time. If you need to leave at 4pm, start getting ready by 3:15. Set reminders for both.
- Create routine rituals that help you orient to time (e.g., a cup of tea at 3pm every day, or a walk at dusk) to provide natural time markers.
- Use event-based prompts instead of time-based ones, when possible. (Example: "After lunch, we'll tidy up," instead of "At 1:30, we'll tidy up.")
- Use checklists with estimated time durations next to each task to increase time awareness (e.g., shower—10 min. Get dressed—5 min).
- Give grace when time blindness disrupts plans. Support and compassion work far better than shame.
- Use shared calendars with alerts if coordinating with others—this is especially helpful for family, partners, or coworkers.

Radical Acceptance:

For a long time, I treated my time blindness like something I could conquer with more discipline. I thought if I tried harder, set more intentions, got the right planner, or cared enough, I'd finally be able to manage time like everyone else. But I kept slipping, forgetting, scrambling—and feeling ashamed. The turning point came when I stopped viewing it as a failure and started seeing it as a neurological difference. My brain simply doesn't track time the same way.

Radical acceptance doesn't mean giving up or lowering expectations. It means I build in supports because I know how my brain works. It means I don't waste energy pretending I can just willpower my way into perfect time management. I use tools, strategies, and lots of alarms. And I let go of the shame that used to come with that. I'm not lazy, flaky, or careless. I'm someone whose brain experiences time differently—and I am finally allowing myself to treat that difference with compassion instead of criticism.

Closing Thoughts

My Dearest Reader,

I'm still learning. I still get confused and miss things. I don't know everything. But I'm no longer building my life on guesswork and survival. Now, I build with awareness— brick by brick, blueprint in hand. I understand what sets me up for collapse and what helps me feel safe. More than anything, I've learned that being neurodivergent doesn't mean I'm broken. It means I need a structure that honors how I work.

My blueprint isn't just about avoiding pain. It's about creating a life that doesn't crumble every time the wind picks up or the pressure builds. I used to live in a delicate and improvised straw house that was constantly on the verge of collapse. Half the time, I didn't even know we were in a storm. I just kept patching walls and bracing for impact.

But now I build with bricks and support beams that make sense for how I am, not how I thought I should be.

Understanding my neurodivergence didn't just change how I live—it changed how I parent, love, and belong. It gave me language, context, and compassion, not only for myself, but for others whose wiring is also misunderstood.

My blueprint became my foundation. It's not perfect. It still shifts and flexes as life unfolds. But it's solid and it's mine. For the first time, I trust that it will hold no matter the weather. If your blueprint is still being drawn up, or is buried beneath old wreckage, know this:

There is nothing wrong with your wiring.

You don't need to be rebuilt, just re-understood.

Start with one brick, and go from there.

With Love,

Lish

About the Author & Further Support

Lish Greiner is a late-diagnosed neurodivergent adult and the parent of a neurodivergent child. She is an author, advocate, and educator who uses her lived experience to help others understand the language, patterns, and inner workings of neurodivergent life.

Through **Neurodivergent Compass**, Lish offers resources that support individuals, families, and partners navigating ADHD, Autism, PDA, sensory processing differences, and the many layers of neurodivergent identity.

Books & Workbooks

Explore Lish's growing library, including:

- *Living in the Straw House That Undiagnosed Neurodivergence Built* (Memoir)
- *From Straw House to Brick House* Workbook Series
    - For Parents
    - For Self-Understanding
    - For Neurotypical Partners
- Upcoming titles, including the *Balanced Badass* Cookbook

Services

Lish offers:

- Lived-experience–based education & guidance
- The Wired Differently Series
- Neurodivergent-informed mentoring

- Workshops & group sessions
- Speaking engagements and community presentations

Visit the website for current offerings and scheduling.

Connect & Learn More

Website: neurodivergentcompass.com
Email: audhdlish@gmail.com
Social: @NeurodivergentCompass on Facebook

A Final Note

Thank you for reading this book. If these pages helped you feel seen, validated, or less alone, your presence here matters more than you know. May this be the beginning of building your own brick-house life—one defined by understanding, compassion, and the freedom to exist as you are.

Made in the USA
Coppell, TX
20 February 2026